Count Me In!

The 'Innovative Learning for All' Series

Series editor: Professor Paul Cooper

The 'Innovative Learning for All' series features accessible books that reveal how schools and educators can meet the needs of vulnerable students, encouraging them to engage in learning and to feel confident in the classroom. Grounded in the latest innovative practice and research, these books offer positive guidance on improving the educational standards for all children by ensuring the most vulnerable are supported.

also in the series

Promoting Emotional Education
Engaging Children and Young People with Social, Emotional and Behavioural Difficulties
Edited by Carmel Cefai and Paul Cooper
ISBN 978 1 84310 996 9

Promoting Resilience in the Classroom
A Guide to Developing Pupils' Emotional and Cognitive Skills
Carmel Cefai
Foreword by Paul Cooper
ISBN 978 1 84310 565 7

Nurture Groups in School and at Home
Connecting with Children with Social, Emotional and Behavioural Difficulties
Paul Cooper and Yonca Tiknaz
ISBN 978 1 84310 528 2

of related interest

Addressing the Unproductive Classroom Behaviours of Students with Special Needs
Steve Chinn
ISBN 978 1 84905 050 0

Making the Move
A Guide for Schools and Parents on the Transfer of Pupils with Autism Spectrum Disorders (ASDs) from Primary to Secondary Schools
K.I. Al-Ghani and Lynda Kenward
Illustrated by Haitham Al-Ghani
ISBN 978 1 84310 934 1

Quick, Easy and Effective Behaviour Management Ideas for the Classroom
Nicola S. Morgan
ISBN 978 1 84310 951 8

Helping Kids and Teens with ADHD in School
A Workbook for Classroom Support and Managing Transitions
Joanne Steer and Kate Horstmann
Illustrated by Jason Edwards
ISBN 978 1 84310 663 0

Street Wise
A Programme for Educating Young People about Citizenship, Rights, Responsibilities and the Law
Sam Frankel
Foreword by Bishop Tim Stevens
ISBN 978 1 84310 680 7

Count Me In!

Ideas for Actively Engaging Students in Inclusive Classrooms

Richard Rose
and Michael Shevlin

Foreword by
Paul Cooper

Jessica Kingsley Publishers
London and Philadelphia

First published in 2010
by Jessica Kingsley Publishers
116 Pentonville Road
London N1 9JB, UK
and
400 Market Street, Suite 400
Philadelphia, PA 19106, USA

www.jkp.com

Library of Congress Cataloging in Publication Data
Rose, Richard, 1953-
  Count me in! : ideas for actively engaging students in the inclusive classroom / Richard Rose and Michael Shevlin ; foreword by Paul Cooper.
    p. cm.
  Includes bibliographical references and index.
  ISBN 978-1-84310-955-6 (alk. paper)
  1. Inclusive education. 2. Mainstreaming in education--Great Britain. 3. Learning disabled children--Education--Great Britain. I. Shevlin, Michael. II. Title.
  LC1203.G7R67 2010
  371.9'046--dc22
                                    2009047429

British Library Cataloguing in Publication Data
A CIP catalogue record for this book is available from the British Library

ISBN 978 1 84310 955 6

Printed and bound in Great Britain by
MPG Books Group, Cornwall

Acknowledgements

This book draws extensively upon not only our own research, but also that of our colleagues who work to ensure that the voices of young people are heard both through the research process and in their classrooms. We are grateful to all these colleagues and in particular we wish to acknowledge the work of:

Yvonne Barnes-Holmes	Barry Groom
Sheena Bell	Marie Howley
Steve Cullingford-Agnew	Kyffin Jones
Cristina Devecchi	Mike Quane
Mary Doveston	Ger Scanlon
Annie Fergusson	Andy Smith
Paula Flynn	Bernie Smyth
Philip Garner	Miriam Twomey
Sue Griffiths	

Most of all, we are grateful to all those young people with whom we have had the pleasure to work as partners during our recent years of research in this area.

Richard Rose and Michael Shevlin

Contents

Case studies

Series Editor's Foreword

The twin needs to raise educational standards for all and to improve access to educational opportunities for the most vulnerable members of society continue to be major challenges facing educators throughout the world.

A crucial factor that can be both a cause and effect of educational failure is 'attachment to school' (Smith 2006). This can be defined as how committed to and engaged with school students are. Students who have a strong attachment to school have feelings of attachment to teachers and believe that success in school will lead to significant rewards in later life. Weak attachment to school is characterized by indifference or hostility towards teachers and scepticism about the value of schooling, and can lead to disaffection and alienation.

Innovative Learning for All offers a series of publications which consider ways in which schools in the 21st century can address the needs of vulnerable students and contribute to their effective attachment to school and engagement with educational opportunities. Each author in the series offers insights into different ways in which these goals can be achieved by drawing on the best available, and in some cases original, research evidence. At the heart of the series is the shared view that educational standards for everyone will improve if we focus our efforts on promoting the educational engagement of the most vulnerable. There is also a strong consensus around the need to value all children and young people as individuals and to maintain a commitment to their positive growth, and for these values to be translated into practical support.

This is not to say that education is a cure all for the dysfunctions of society. Far from it, the ideas and practices described in this series depend upon political will and government action to achieve their best. It follows, therefore, that the authors in this series all hope that some of the ideas that they put forward will contribute to both the thinking and practice of educators as well as politicians.

Paul Cooper, University of Leicester

REFERENCES

Smith, D. (2006) *School Experience and Delinquency at Ages 13 to 16*. Edinburgh: Centre for Law and Society, University of Edinburgh.

Introduction

Schools change. They do so in part in response to developments in the society in which we live and in the context of other political, technological and socio-economic changes. A teacher from 40 years ago visiting a classroom today would certainly recognize much of what they saw. In particular the professional commitment of teachers to their pupils, the well-prepared and planned lessons, the use of basic pedagogical skills involving questioning pupils, promoting discussion and checking learning would all be familiar. Less so might be the use of information technology such as interactive whiteboards and visualizers or the use of additional adults such as teaching assistants in classrooms. Similarly, the attention given to personalizing learning and the endeavours made to include pupils with a diverse range of learning and behaviour needs may be seen to have brought increased demands to the classroom of the 21st century.

Whilst teachers in the past would have been familiar with many of the challenges posed by pupils with special educational needs, in today's classrooms the pressure to be seen to address these needs may be considerably greater than before. The promotion of inclusive schooling, which is a welcome development from a period in which many pupils were excluded and denied opportunities for learning, has undoubtedly come with new challenges as well as providing exciting learning opportunities. The demands upon teachers are probably greater now than at any time previously in the modern era.

The reasons for change and the influences upon schools are often positive. The development of technology has, for example, provided some pupils with a means of accessing the curriculum and learning that would previously have been unavailable. A pupil using an adapted keyboard that enables him to express his ideas in written form, or the child who has access to a communication board which enables her to ask for assistance and participate in lessons, has advantages that in previous years would not have been available. Visit many classrooms today and it is possible to see children using less technologically advanced support programmes, such as social stories or visual cue cards, which were previously unknown in the majority of mainstream schools. The commitment of teachers to develop innovative approaches to teaching and learning, accompanied by a desire to ensure that pupils who have previously been marginalized are included, has been a feature of the late 20th and early 21st centuries. The professionalism and dedication of teachers has beyond doubt been a major factor not only in addressing change, but also in taking the lead in showing how technological and other advances may be used for the benefits of all learners.

Other changes in schools have not been so readily welcomed. The often negative portrayal of teachers and schools in the media and the perpetual imposition of new government initiatives have taken their toll upon the teaching profession. When teachers and pupils achieve success in schools, this is often accepted only begrudgingly by a media which suggests that examinations have become easier or the curriculum fails to address the fundamentals of traditional learning. Furthermore, education has become an easy target for party politicians intent on scoring points against each other by making claims and counter-claims about the quality of teaching and the efficacy of the current schooling system.

Amidst all this change and debate are the teachers and their pupils who are at the sharp end of our education system where the daily round of lessons are delivered and received. Schools are for the most part orderly places where the social and academic demands are met with enthusiasm and good will. However, teachers, who are generally by nature creative and innovative individuals, have been required too often to be reactive in their response to new and often untried initiatives. In many instances the professional initiative of teachers has been undermined and their creativity arrested. Yet, despite this, the majority of our schools continue to flourish and to provide an excellent standard of education to pupils with a diverse range of needs and abilities. Where schools succeed we would suggest that this is directly as a result of the effectiveness of teachers despite the pressures placed upon them to adopt a raft of new initiatives and to adapt their teaching accordingly.

Pupils in schools have not been exempt from the pressures that have come with change. The very public scrutiny of academic attainment through league tables and well publicized opinions with regard to what are seen as minimum performance outcomes for school leavers leave pupils in no doubt about their own perceived academic standing. Those pupils who achieve high standards find the veracity of their success challenged in the media, and for those who struggle to attain the highest outcomes education can become a disheartening experience. Far from feeling supported in their learning, a significant number of young people see themselves disenfranchised and disillusioned by the expectations placed upon them. A small number of these pupils will react by kicking against the authority of our schooling system, whilst others will withdraw, seeing schooling and notions of lifelong learning as an irrelevance for them.

The media-driven perception that schools are out of control and that ill-discipline and disruptive behaviour dominates adds to the frustrations of teachers and pupils alike. At the heart of the debate surrounding behaviour in schools lies the perception that children lack the respect for adults that was commonly expected in the past. Children, we are told, no longer know how to behave, and teachers lack the skills to instil discipline in schools. Coupled with this, the authority of the teacher is said to have been undermined by the shifting social mores of a society dominated by political correctness and a general disrespect for authority. Many critics of today's schools hark back to a golden era when teachers were held in higher esteem and pupils arrived at school eager to learn and in awe of those who taught them. However, the evidence that such a time existed is at best flimsy and is perpetuated for the most part by those who have little real understanding of the ways in which schools have operated in the recent past.

An informed debate about standards in education and the nature of schooling should always be welcomed. An improved understanding of how children learn and the most effective approaches to teaching and school management should always provide a focus for teachers, education policy makers and researchers alike. We would contend that a critical factor in any such discourse should be an endeavour to understand how the relationships between teachers and their pupils can be developed to promote effective learning, foster positive attitudes and behaviours and enhance the social fabric of schools. The teacher and pupil relationship is, and always has been, the most critical factor in determining whether pupils succeed or fail in schools. Pupils who feel secure, valued and respected are more likely to respond positively to learning and to accept the essential authority which needs to influence the ethos of all schools.

Our motivations for writing this book come from our belief that a positive pupil and teacher relationship is the most essential underpinning factor in successful schools. This belief is founded upon our experiences of working over many years in schools with teachers, pupils and parents and builds on the research we have undertaken to examine those influences that determine whether pupils feel included in or excluded from the education system. Much of our work has been conducted with pupils who are described as having special educational needs or have been marginalized within both education and wider society.

We have drawn extensively upon this experience, but in this book we suggest that the principles discussed within its pages are generic and may be applied to learners of all abilities and in any educational system. The focus of our research has been upon the ways in which pupils accept some responsibility for their own learning, rather than expecting adults, and particularly teachers, to provide for all their needs. If teachers are able to achieve this with those pupils who are seen to be challenging our education system, as we will demonstrate here, then it is surely possible for all young people in our schools.

For many young people with special educational needs a culture of dependency has been the norm. However, many of the practices we have seen deployed by teachers that we describe in this book have attempted to increase pupil independence by ensuring that they are capable of making choices and decisions that affect their lives and learning and also have a positive impact upon their attitudes and behaviours.

The book is about pupil involvement and advocates teaching approaches that put them at the heart of all decision-making processes. This includes involvement in planning for the teaching they will receive, assessing their own learning outcomes, negotiating personal targets and analysing their own performance. In calling for a clearer partnership between pupils and their teachers we are not suggesting a lessening of the authority of the teacher. We are rather suggesting that the promotion of such partnerships is more likely to enhance the respect of pupils for teachers and encourage the acceptance of increased responsibility by pupils for their personal learning outcomes.

Furthermore, we suggest that the concerns expressed in many quarters about pupil behaviour are more likely to be addressed through the promotion of pupil involvement than through the imposition of authoritarian or punitive measures. In so doing we know that for some teachers and for many policy makers this is a proposition with which they will feel uncomfortable and that in some instances they will be unwilling to be convinced. We are also conscious that this acceptance may become even more difficult when we attempt to apply the principles of developing partnerships for learning with pupils described as having special educational needs.

Pupils with disabilities, those with learning difficulties or others who are labelled as troubled, or more often troublesome, continue to present as a challenge within our schools. Indeed, it would be foolish to suggest that such pupils do not at times give cause for concern and that they may be demanding of additional teacher time and, in some instances, other resources. However, evidence suggests that these pupils are often subjected to low expectations and negative attitudes, which results in their exclusion from many of the learning opportunities others take for granted. Our experiences, both as teachers and researchers, have led us to believe that the more we raise our expectations of all pupils, including those with special educational needs, the more likely that they will succeed as learners and develop as individuals. Listening to the voices of young people reflecting upon their educational experiences through research such as the 'Encouraging Voices Project' (Shevlin and Rose 2003) has shown us that we have much to learn from those who have experienced marginalization or exclusion from education systems.

However, listening to voices is only a starting point for teachers who are committed to improving the learning opportunities of their pupils. There is an imperative which demands that we take actions to seek a better understanding of the ways in which we can achieve a more equitable education system for the benefits of all pupils. Simply listening is not enough; we must now take note of the experiences of a generation of young people who have progressed through school at a time when both the social and educational inclusion agenda has been heralded as a priority within our society, and ensure that what we have learned influences our practice and benefits the current pupils in our schools. By so doing we will not only be supporting progress towards independence for pupils who have until recently been seen as likely to require long-term support well beyond school-leaving age, but will also be affording teachers a chance to foster more positive relationships with their pupils and maintain higher expectations of behaviour and learning.

This book draws not only on our own experiences, but also those of teachers with whom we have worked over a number of years. Within the book we present case studies demonstrating how teachers have adopted practices that have encouraged greater pupil participation. In so doing we discuss the benefits to be gained through greater pupil involvement, not only for the individual pupils concerned but also for their peers and for teachers.

At no point do we suggest that encouraging pupil participation is easy. We recognize that for many pupils learning, and indeed even being within a school environment, can be a difficult and far from satisfying experience. Similarly, we acknowledge that for many teachers adopting practices that encourage greater pupil autonomy may at first appear problematic or even threatening. A commitment to greater pupil involvement may make additional demands upon teachers in terms of time and resource management, and many of the benefits to be gained will not be achieved overnight. We would, however, suggest that the endeavours made in this direction will encourage pupils to become more focused on their learning, will enable them to accept greater responsibility for their learning and will support the development of positive behaviours.

Whilst the book draws upon our own experiences and those of teacher colleagues, it calls particularly upon the views, experiences and ideas of many young people with whom it has been our privilege to work. The text is illustrated throughout with quotations from children and young people whose words have been used without any modification on our part. We have similarly examined the views expressed by pupils in a broader literature reporting the research of colleagues who have been engaged in studies of pupil involvement over the past ten years. A growing corpus of literature in this area has demonstrated an increased commitment on the part of researchers, teachers and, in some instances, policy makers to appreciate the insights that can be gained from listening to young people in schools.

Above all, this book aims to examine the practicalities of pupil involvement and to demonstrate the exciting work of teachers and pupils who, through working closely in partnership, have explored ways of overcoming learning difficulties and in so doing have learned from each other. Our knowledge of how children learn most effectively may still be at an early stage of its evolution; we believe that progress towards greater understanding will be achieved through maintaining an effective dialogue between teachers and their pupils.

REFERENCES

Shevlin, M. and Rose, R. (eds) (2003) *Encouraging Voices: Respecting the Insights of Young People Who Have Been Marginalised.* Dublin: National Disability Authority.

CHAPTER 1

Exploring the Teacher and Student Relationship: Creating a Partnership for Learning

Effective teaching is built around relationships that foster trust and confidence, build self-esteem and encourage curiosity and an enthusiasm for learning. Evidence suggests that the relationships established between teachers and their pupils are critical in enabling the creation of positive learning environments and that where these relationships break down effective teaching and learning becomes difficult (O'Brien 1998; Pianta and Stuhlman 2004). It therefore follows that time devoted to considering the development of positive teacher and pupil relationships may be critical in enabling all parties to gain maximum benefits from schooling.

Recent research in the United States has indicated how when improvements were made in adult and child relationships in kindergarten settings there was a corresponding growth in learning confidence in children (Mashburn *et al.* 2008). Similar findings from other studies (Griffiths and Davis 1995) emphasize that time spent in developing clearly defined principles around teacher and pupil interactions may well reap benefits in terms of both social and academic performance.

Children are keen to have opportunities to discover the world around them and are 'born poised to learn' (Nutbrown 1996, p.102). However, unless children are provided with an element of freedom and space and a lack of pressure, many will be turned off learning and will fail to thrive in schools. Children need 'real challenge' in their lives if they are to develop as effective learners, and the role of educators is to ensure that all of these essential elements are created in classrooms, in order to enable children to gain confidence and an enthusiasm for learning (Nutbrown 1996).

In many respects we can see that this stance throws down a challenge to teachers and, more especially, to policy makers. It asks them to consider how they might define the fine balance between maintaining well-ordered classrooms and providing exciting and stimulating opportunities for children to learn, with an element of freedom and autonomy. In effect, we are asked to review the role of the teacher and those classroom relationships which are at the core of learning. Within this book we intend to place the teacher and pupil relationship at the heart of our discussion in order to identify the ways in which this may be developed to promote a more inclusive learning environment.

Relationships between teachers and pupils have inevitably evolved to reflect wider societal changes over time. Classrooms today, whilst undoubtedly maintaining many of the characteristics of earlier learning environments, have certainly changed as different approaches to pedagogy and the availability of new resources and teaching materials have become available. The notion that teaching and learning have remained static or that there was some kind of golden era in which the rules of teacher and student interaction were firmly established is a false premise and one which teachers need to challenge. Whilst there are characteristics of effective teaching, centred upon organization, knowledge and classroom management skills, which have always been essential and have set the good teacher apart from those who are less adequate, the cultural and social contexts of classrooms have gradually changed to reflect developments in society as a whole. Teachers still have a duty to instil in their learners those moral and intellectual values that equip them to play a role as citizens within the communities in which they will live. However, the ways in which this may be achieved will continue to provide a focus for debate so long as schools exist. Any teacher from the past who visited one of today's classrooms would undoubtedly see features and characteristics they would recognize. It is equally certain that they would be surprised by some of the actions they witnessed, not least in respect of the teacher and pupil relationship.

The nature of that relationship is worthy of further consideration in a book that is concerned to explore the ways in which pupils may play a more influential role in understanding and managing their own learning needs. Over the years many books have been devoted to the nature of teaching, and efforts have been made to deconstruct the skills teachers require in order to be effective. Whilst aspects of classroom management and pedagogy have always provided a lively focus for debate, on one point there appears to be some consensus. Pupils respond best to those teachers for whom they have respect, generally wishing to please them by working hard to achieve tasks the teacher sets. By contrast, where pupils lack this respect, they are less likely to respond positively and in extremes will behave badly and adopt a negative stance towards learning.

What is then clear is the necessity for teachers to demonstrate to their pupils that they care for them, have their best interests at heart and will do their utmost to support them in their learning. This does not imply that the teacher needs to become the 'best friend' of the pupil or try to win the learner over by adopting aspects of youth culture. Indeed, such attempts, far from gaining the respect of the pupil, are likely to be interpreted as false and to result in the contempt rather than respect of the learner. However, an understanding of the ways in which children view teachers can be informative and may assist us in our constant review of the teacher's role.

WHAT DO CHILDREN TELL US ABOUT THEIR TEACHERS?

Inevitably, the close interactions between teachers and their pupils result in fairly strong opinions being expressed about teaching and the role of teachers. Some students provide astute insights into the challenges that exist when trying to develop a good working relationship between the teacher and his or her pupils. This is illustrated by the following quotation taken from Burke and Grosvenor (2003), who collected the views of large numbers of school pupils on many aspects of life at school.

> Rightly or wrongly, the power relationships between pupils and teachers are unequal in most schools, but I think that teachers frequently abuse their authority. It is often seen as acceptable for the young to be treated with disrespect or to be humiliated. There is a very pronounced 'respect double standard' in schools, which manifests itself in the way pupils are spoken to... A 'ticking off' tends to have more to do with power and punishment than with logic or negotiation... Many of the ritualised details of school are degrading and unnecessary. For instance, it is quite common for a teacher to insist that a class stand up in his/her presence, until he/she has the condescension to allow them to sit! Teachers are addressed by titles, rather than their first names – some even insist on being called 'sir'. I can see no benefit in this outdated habit. In general, pupils are expected to be deferent,

while teachers are allowed to be unpleasant, high handed and often unreasonable.

Lorna, aged 14, Ipswich

We are not suggesting that Lorna's view of teachers is in any way representative of teenage pupils as a whole. What is clear from this quotation is that she is an articulate and thoughtful young lady who has clear ideas about teacher and pupil relationships and their impact upon herself as a learner. The views expressed by Lorna and the force with which she articulates them may well have challenged teachers in the past. We may, however, interpret them as a reflection of the changes that have taken place in society as a whole. Notions of deference to figures of authority, which may have pervaded in earlier times, have been replaced by a more reciprocal idea that asserts that respect should be earned and is a two-way process.

There are undoubtedly many teachers, parents and politicians who will feel that a teacher relationship from a previous era, one in which respect was 'commanded' and where pupils saw the authority of the teacher as paramount in the classroom, has been undermined by a change in societal standards. Such a debate undoubtedly has its place and will continue to occupy column inches in the press for many years to come. In this book we would prefer to reflect upon classrooms as they are today and to see how positive relationships between teachers and pupils can be fostered for the benefit of learning. In exploring these issues we believe that the crucial role of the teacher requires support from managers and policy makers who recognize that the very process of teaching and learning is dependent upon the establishment of good relationships and a clarification of roles.

Unfortunately, in recent years, a technocratic view of teaching that has in some instances portrayed teachers as simple purveyors of prescribed and formulaic information has failed to acknowledge those interpersonal skills so essential to teaching quality. We are often told that everyone remembers a good teacher. This is indeed true. It is of particular interest to note that when asked about memorable teachers who influenced their lives most people highlight the inspiration that emanated from the relationship skills of these individuals as much as from their subject knowledge. We would suggest that both subject knowledge and the ability to form positive relationships with pupils are important factors in identifying teacher effectiveness.

Pupils are often perceptive about those teacher actions that have enabled them to develop both academically and personally. By listening to their voices we have an opportunity to learn about our own role as teachers and to reflect upon how we might develop our practice in order to support learning. It is evident that many young people are able to afford insights into those teacher actions, that either supported or inhibited learning.

> There were one or two [teachers] that helped. The rest didn't seem to give a toss. One teacher I respected was patient with students if there was a problem. He would talk to you in private versus in front [of the class]. There was mutual respect. I instantly knew he could be respected and was trustworthy. (pupil cited in Hornby and Witte 2008, p.105)

This student clearly experienced both positive and negative relationships with teachers. Of particular note is the use of terms such as 'respected' and 'trustworthy' in this quotation. Here we have a pupil who is clearly stating what it is he values in a teacher and who demonstrates a willingness to respond in a positive manner when a teacher behaves in a particular way. The positive influence which teachers can have upon pupils' views of school is evident in the view of a pupil from an English secondary school:

> There is always courses, things to do after school. The teachers are dedicated to you, they like gives you work on the plate. It is not like some teachers where they are just not really bothered about your education, most of these teachers are really bothered about your education. (pupil cited in Rose and Shelvin 2007, p.36)

In this case we see evidence of a student who recognizes and appreciates the dedication of his teachers and is therefore likely to respond to them in a positive manner.

CHILDREN IN SOCIETY

Children often receive a bad press. The media appears to prefer to paint a picture of children in our society who are out of control and causing distress, rather than seeking stories depicting young people in a positive light. We would contend that the vast majority of young people are well-adjusted, well-behaved members of our society who want to succeed and make a contribution to their communities.

It has been suggested that children are often perceived as being in need of improvement and that the immaturity which is an inevitable factor of childhood, rather than being seen as an essential state of transition is regarded as an inconvenience needing to be addressed. Furthermore, we need to regard childhood as a stage of development unique in terms of characteristics that need to be appreciated in their own right (Loreman 2009). We should therefore perhaps consider childhood as a distinct period of life, which cannot be hurried through, and that a desire to move quickly to establishing mature behaviours may in fact undermine the very development that we seek. Our approach to managing this stage of transition from immaturity to maturity should not be by exercising control in a way that suppresses the ability of children to become effective independent decision makers or to understand their own responsibilities in the world. When children are steered as opposed to being offered guidance and when they are discouraged from expressing their own ideas in order to think about their own behaviours, they often become restive and in some instances become difficult to work with in classrooms.

Children respond positively to the relationships they form with those closest to them, and it takes time for them to extend these early bonds to those who may be perceived as being at a greater distance. Also the essential egotistic nature of childhood is such that children will inevitably at the commencement of a relationship seek to see what benefits might accrue to themselves. It is suggested that the adult who is able to demonstrate affection, respect and love towards a child is most likely to develop a relationship in which the child comes to reciprocate these feelings and show a willingness to engage in activity that is of mutual benefit (Bronfenbrenner 1979).

There is, of course, plenty of evidence to show that when relationships do not begin well this may result in tensions and mutual distrust. The teacher and pupil relationship is amongst the most complex with which a child must learn to engage. Unlike the naturally bonded relationships that occur in most families, or those based upon choice, which characterize friendships, the relationship a child has with a teacher is imposed. This is of course inevitable. Schools must allocate pupils to classes and must also utilize the expertise and experience of teachers for the benefit of the majority of pupils. However, the very fact that teachers and pupils are brought together in this way requires that efforts should be made to develop a relationship that affords benefits to both parties.

The idea of 'agency', which is defined as an appreciation of children's capacity to understand, act upon and influence their world, has received considerable attention in recent years (Mayall 2002; Waller 2009). Children are known to develop an early capacity to express their emotions and ideas and it has been suggested that by harnessing these skills teachers are more likely to enable them to become effective learners. Teachers and other adults should perhaps assume a level of competence rather than incompetence in children, which may enable them to become more conversant with their own abilities and to translate this into knowledge into an appreciation of how they can influence and support their own learning (Penrose *et al* 2001).

Such a concept is of course challenging and requires that teachers analyse their own classroom actions in order to see how they might best facilitate pupils becoming more fully engaged in the management of their own learning. However, evidence suggests that most teachers enjoy such challenges and are innovative in finding approaches that ensure the effective learning of their pupils.

In many respects teachers need to act as advocates for the pupils in their charge. Whereas certain factions of society perpetuate a negative view of young people, teachers have an opportunity to see all aspects of their pupils' characteristics and also have the ability to influence and shape these. The pupil who looks up to his teacher, respects him and relates to him positively is more likely to carry this view of adults and people in positions of responsibility beyond the school gate. In many ways teachers may not be representative of adults in society as a whole. Their professional development, commitment and vocation places them in a unique position to understand young people and to assist them in developing the attitudes and beliefs that they will take with them into their communities. For this reason a consideration of the nature of teacher and pupil relationships is critical to our understanding of the teaching and learning process.

AN EMPHASIS UPON LEARNING AND EFFECTIVE SCHOOLS

Promoting the involvement of pupils in decision making is not about giving them the upper hand in the classroom. Rather it is about increasing the responsibilities that they take for their own learning. Pupils learn best when they see the relevance of what is being taught. They respond to teaching when they can see the benefits to be gained from learning and have an understanding of teacher expectations. These expectations need to be articulated by the teacher and fully understood by the pupil. This requires the creation of time for dialogue and an emphasis upon enabling pupils to rationalize and appreciate the importance of classroom activity.

Teachers spend a lot of time on assessing the needs of pupils and trying to understand how best to enable them to learn. A focus upon academic outcomes has, understandably, dominated the discourse in this area. A curriculum that emphasizes subject content and places value upon the testing of learning outcomes in relation to academic attainment inevitably leads the teacher to focus upon these as opposed to taking a more holistic view of the pupil.

The skills required to deliver the curriculum are considerable and present a challenge to all teachers. Understanding the conditions required for effective learning makes even more demands upon the professionalism of the teacher. Teacher effectiveness has been discussed for as long as schools have existed, and lists identifying the attributes of effective teachers abound (Dean 1994; Department for Education and Skills 2005; Reid, Hopkins and Holly 1987). Such lists quite rightly emphasize the need for teachers to have good organizational skills, to be able to convey difficult concepts in a way that pupils can understand, to adopt positive discipline strategies and to be able to manage time efficiently. These skills and attributes undoubtedly contribute to the teacher being able to provide good learning experiences to their pupils. However, each of these must be underpinned by a foundation of positive teacher and pupil relationship.

For over a decade it has been acknowledged that there is a need to place greater emphasis upon understanding the teacher and student relationship when considering school effectiveness (Reynolds and Teddlie 2000). This belief that such relationships impact upon the effectiveness of schools is reinforced through legislation and procedure governing the ways in which schools operate today.

In inspecting schools the Office for Standards in Education (Ofsted) has recognized the value of seeking the views of pupils on the quality of the education they receive. Similarly, a demand to listen to pupil voices has been incorporated into educational policy including the Special Needs Code of Practice (Department for Education and Skills 2001). It is now common practice for schools to have pupil representation on their governing bodies, and schools councils have been a feature for many years. A move away from a system in which the pupil is perceived simply as a recipient of learning, to one where a greater recognition of their abilities to take more responsibility for their own performance, has been accepted in the most effective schools.

SUMMARY

In this chapter we have:

- considered the teacher and pupil relationship and the demands of the 21st century classroom
- examined perceptions of children and childhood and how these influence attitudes
- listened to what children tell us about teachers
- considered the imperative for listening to the voices of young people in schools.

REFERENCES

Bronfenbrenner, U. (1979) *The Ecology of Human Development: Experiments by Nature and Design.* Cambridge, MA: Harvard University Press.

Burke, C. and Grosvenor, I. (2003) *The School I'd Like.* London: Routledge.

Dean, J. (1994) *Organising Learning in the Primary School Classroom.* London: Routledge.

Department for Education and Skills (2001) *Special Needs Code of Practice.* London: HMSO.

Department for Education and Skills (2005) *Excellent Teachers.* Nottingham: DfES.

Griffiths, M. and Davis, C. (1995) *In Fairness to Children.* London: David Fulton.

Hornby, G, and Witte, C. (2008) 'Looking back on school – the views of adult graduates of a residential special school for children with emotional and behavioural difficulties.' *British Journal of Special Education 35,* 2, 102–107.

Loreman, T. (2009) *Respecting Childhood.* London: Continuum.

Mashburn, A., Pianta, R., Hamre, B., Downer, J., Barbarin, O., Bryant, D., Burchinal, M., Early, D. and Howes, C. (2008) 'Measures of classroom quality in prekindergarten and children's development of academic, language, and social skills.' *Child Development 79,* 3, 732–749.

Mayall, B. (2002) *Towards a Sociology of Childhood: Thinking from Children's Lives.* Buckingham: Open University Press.

Nutbrown, C. (1996) *Children's Rights and Early Education.* London: Paul Chapman.

O'Brien, T. (1998) *Promoting Positive Behaviour.* London: David Fulton.

Penrose, V., Thomas, G. and Greed, C. (2001) 'Designing inclusive schools: how can children be involved?' *Support for Learning 16,* 2, 87–91.

Pianta, R. and Stuhlman, M. (2004) 'Teacher-child relationships and children's success in the first years of school.' *School Psychology Review 33,* 3, 444–458.

Reid, K., Hopkins, D. and Holly, P. (1987) *Towards the Effective School.* Oxford: Blackwell.

Reynolds, D. and Teddlie, C. (2000) 'The Future Agenda for School Effectiveness Research.' In C. Teddlie and D. Reynolds (eds) *The International Handbook of School Effectiveness Research.* London: Falmer.

Rose, R. and Shevlin, M. (2007) *Capable or not? Who decides? Exploring the implications for children and young people with special educational needs.* Irish Association of Teachers in Special Education (IATSE) International Conference, Drumcondra, Dublin, 7th–9th June.

Waller, T. (2009) *An Introduction to Early Childhood* (2nd edition). London: Sage.

CHAPTER 2

Barriers to Participation

While substantial attention has been given to developing an infrastructure to support the development of inclusive learning environments, there has been relatively little focus on the experiences of the children and young people who have disabilities and/or special educational needs within school settings. This lack of attention impacts not only on children and young people with special needs themselves, but also on pupils more generally. While this group present their own particular, and varied, challenges to effective teaching and learning, we find that many of the techniques and approaches that work with them for fostering supportive learning environments will work with all pupils. So listening to and learning from children with disabilities and other special needs is important for improving classroom participation for all.

It has generally been assumed that children and young people with disabilities and for special educational needs will automatically benefit from the mainstream environment and social contact with their peer group. It was initially believed that placement within mainstream schools would guarantee that they were fully included in school life. However, this expectation did not take sufficient account of the complex set of intersecting factors that shape school life for them. These factors can include a lack of awareness of how societal attitudes towards disability and special educational needs can influence the interactions of these young people with their peer group and their teachers, combined with a school belief that their knowledge and experience of these issues are limited.

Within this chapter we will examine the nature of the barriers that children and young people with disabilities and/or special educational needs can experience within school. These barriers can consist of inadequate school knowledge and capacity to respond to individual learning needs.

Gaining initial and ongoing access to school, classroom life, curriculum and social relationships can be particularly problematic for these children and young people. We will explore these issues and incorporate their perspectives on experiences of school. To conclude, we will provide a case study that examines the exclusion of a child from formal schooling and the subsequent efforts to include him in meaningful learning.

Many studies have addressed the challenges schools, teachers and support staff encounter in developing appropriate provision for children and young people who have a disability and/or special educational need. However, it is only more recently that research has begun to address this imbalance through direct consultation with the young people concerned and has ascertained the real-life school experiences of these young people (Kenny *et al.* 2003; Watson *et al.* 1999). This chapter draws extensively on this research and the voices of those young people.

GAINING ACCESS: A SOCIAL AND PERSONAL EXPERIENCE

Achieving access and participation in school life is usually a multi-layered process that is often implicit and relatively seamless for the majority of children. However, for children and young people with disabilities and/or special educational needs this process is not straightforward. An obvious prerequisite for such access is being present and engaged where the curriculum is being delivered and wider activities are being pursued. Physical presence and engagement involves a number of levels that include: choice of school; accessing classrooms; using equipment; and participating in curricular and extracurricular activities. From the outset of their school careers children with disabilities and/or special educational needs and their families can face access issues. Entry to school is rarely straightforward and will often be conditional. This is illustrated by the experiences of some families of children who have Down syndrome as they attempted to gain access to their local mainstream school (Kenny *et al.* 2003):

> [The Principal] met Jason a couple of times and said everything was fine. [In June]…he changed his mind. [He sent a teacher to tell the preschool teacher.] She told me. I was in an awful state, crying my eyes out. Put her in a terrible position as well… I went down maybe a week or so later, seemingly the teachers had just decided and that was it, the end of it. (p.70)

> I remember discussing it with a chap I work with who's on the local school management and he said 'there's a place for them' and that really grated on me to the extent that I still remember that expression. This is the thing you have to change. That attitude has to go. (p.67)

These excerpts demonstrate how children with a particular identified condition can be subject to negative attitudes and expectations that present an almost insuperable barrier to actually achieving entry to the school. Parents often have to present their case and hope for a positive response:

> They [the school] were a bit apprehensive – they had never taught a child with Down syndrome. We went up and we actually had a formal meeting with all the staff. Now they were very courteous and very nice...but we had to put our case...they came back to us and said they were prepared to try, see how it goes, all the usual stuff, even though at that time there wasn't any back-up resources, so we tried it. (p.21)

> We live in a very small country area and we know the teacher socially. [My husband] is in the selling business – he literally 'sold' my daughter like a pair of sheets. 'She'll be no trouble blah blah'... (p.18)

Point of entry difficulties can also be encountered by young people with a physical disability as their subject choice was limited by assumptions about capability and physical access issues:

> I was going to go to the carry on one from primary, but the headmistress would not allow me to do home economics or biology. Home economics because in case I might spill something on someone or biology because it was on the top floor so I instantly removed myself from that school and went to another one that would allow me to do the subjects I wanted to do. (Kenny *et al.* 2000, p.22)

Parents of children with disabilities and/or special educational needs often face an ongoing effort to achieve and maintain an appropriate educational experience for their child, which can be particularly problematic at times of transition. Educational choice has limited applicability to these parents and their children as they struggle to access appropriate provision.

Parents find themselves, often reluctantly, acting as advocates for their children in interactions with schools and professional support services. Some parents are frustrated at their lack of participation in educational decision making and what they consider an appropriate response from schools asserting that 'lip service' characterizes school approaches to facilitating their involvement. Transport difficulties have been cited as a major impediment to access by many parents, with some having to take on the responsibility for bringing their child to school over a long distance, which has implications for opportunities for after-school socializing for their child.

While many parents value the understanding and support demonstrated by teachers and support professionals, a substantial number perceive a significant gap between their insights into their own children and the professional perspective, and feel that their views are not given sufficient consideration in the decision-making processes.

Some students with physical disabilities report experiencing substantial difficulties gaining access to at least some teaching spaces (Kenny *et al.* 2000). As one said, if classmates didn't carry him up to second-floor subject classrooms, he 'just didn't go to that class'. Difficulty getting around in the built environment also affected this young person's social relationships with peers:

> The first year or so took me a while to settle in – there was one other person I think with a disability in the school so it was kind of difficult just to basically get around. And asking for help – I found that difficult, I didn't like asking the same person all the time and you know it was difficult finding somebody different every day or you know some people would make a fuss over me and other people wouldn't think. It was a mixture of reactions. (p.25)

As this comment shows, social considerations had become firmly rooted in peer relations. The private needs of young people, such as going to the toilet, sometimes entered the public domain and due to inadequate access other arrangements have to be fashioned:

> If I wanted to go to the toilet, the cubicles were very small; I had to go to the teachers' room. They knew and I had someone outside the door just in case they'd come. It wasn't too bad. (p.23)

The stoicism ('It wasn't too bad') expressed by this speaker appeared to be a common feature of management strategies employed by these young people:

> There were glass fire doors, I couldn't open them. I went to the Principal, I went to everyone and they did nothing… If I wanted to go to the bathroom during class, or if I was carrying something for art, it was a long way. There were really steep ramps and twice I fell. I'd have to wait for someone to help me. But you get used to it after a while. (p.24)

Struggle was a regular characteristic of attempting to access the built environment:

> You had to fight. One girl had spina bifida. And a guy. There was no way he could have done science experiments. I think he ended up leaving – don't know if it was personal reasons or the school. The girl couldn't handle the crowds, 1200 in the school. She left as well…
> (p.24)

ASSUMPTIONS AND EXPECTATIONS

While acknowledging that there are certain differences between young people with disabilities and/or special educational needs and their peer group, it has been observed that these young people often experience socially created and reinforced interpretations of difference and normality that emphasize the view that they were innately passive; and that professionals tend to label them as dependent and qualitatively different from their peers (Watson *et al.* 1999).

This adult perspective is often inextricably linked to the perception that these children are less capable than their peers, with teachers tending to underestimate the capabilities of children with disabilities and/or special educational needs and having lowered expectations for their learning outcomes (Wilson and Jade 1999).

Children and young people with special educational needs are frequently distinguished from their peers by formal and informal processes that can involve identification and assessment procedures, statementing and school arrangements that clearly differentiate them from their peer group (Priestley 2001). These arrangements could involve attending a special unit, being excused from physical education and having the support of a special needs assistant. While these arrangements are not intended to exclude them there is a real risk that unless this process is sensitively managed these children will be viewed in a negative fashion by their peers. Disabled children have been found to be acutely aware of feeling different and being treated differently by their peers and teachers (McArthur *et al.* 2007).

Lowered teacher expectations may have negative impacts on students with dyslexia (Kenny *et al.* 2000):

> If you're dyslexic you won't be going anywhere so let's not bother…
> So there was an attitude that if you have something wrong with you you don't have to reach the same standards others do… I always set

> myself, my standards many times too high because I thought at least
> if you reach high you'll get somewhere. (p.28)

Different teacher expectations appear evident in relation to students with a disability and/or special educational need compared to their peers:

> Well basically the teachers were grand I probably got some special treatment from them if I didn't do my homework they'd be like ok – they wouldn't really mind if I didn't do it whereas the other children they'd... (unpublished transcript)

A student with a physical disability reported similar experiences in that she was treated differently in relation to exam results compared to her peer group:

> If I got bad results in the exams it was try better next time as if... Whereas if anyone else got a bad result there was an in depth... (p.28)

Some teachers, uncertain of themselves in relation to pupils with physical disabilities, can overcompensate and give unwarranted praise for quite ordinary achievements (MacConville 2007). There is also an indication that teacher uncertainty affects their willingness to enable the student to participate in classroom work (Kenny *et al.* 2000):

> In the very start when I went to this school there were one or two teachers you would have your hand raised for the answer and they wouldn't ask in case your wrong or something...uh so annoying but then once they got to know me they realised there was nothing wrong I can answer questions. (unpublished transcript)

According to another student, teachers may only acknowledge students' abilities when demonstrated in formal examinations:

> They did once I got my junior cert results to a certain degree because it went up by nearly two grades in a lot of subjects and some of the teachers were kind of a ok she's telling the truth and then I moved school like I know I moved straight away and the whole thing started again really and am it was all over again. (unpublished transcript)

Students may sometimes feel they lack confidence and support and as a result take examinations at a lower level, as reported by one deaf student:

> Yea I did all pass subjects I wasn't going to take the risk. (unpublished transcript)

PARTICIPATION IN THE CURRICULUM

Subjects that require physical participation appear to be particularly problematic. Adapting to the environment and expectations can be lacking in some situations, as the following remarks bear out (Kenny *et al.* 2000):

> In science, using things on the bench, I just sat down and watched.

> I think most of us were excluded especially in sports – the school wasn't equipped to cope. They tried, but the majority of times you had to stay out.

> The PE teacher let me watch. There was no discrimination.

> [Q: Did they include exercises suited to you?]

> Oh no, no. But he was very good. (p.31)

This last exchange was with a student with a disability whose exclusion was not apparent to himself and he was grateful for a minimal level of involvement.

Exclusion from extracurricular outings is a source of great difficulty for many young people with disabilities and/or special educational needs and this has a consequent impact on social relationships with peers, as another student in the same study reported:

> I would listen to them when they came back – 'You missed a great couple of days, we'd great fun.' Even sitting beside them hearing them laughing, it was laughing at something you didn't understand. I didn't like that. (p.32)

Similar difficulties have been reported for young people with disabilities who miss out on trips because the accommodation is not accessible and this had not been taken into account in preparations (Curtin and Clarke 2005). Some extracurricular activities are dependent on parents providing the necessary support, or sometimes the child is actively excluded when the school perceives that they lack adequate resources to facilitate a trip as, for example, when a child with an autism spectrum disorder (ASD) is involved. Personal dignity can also be compromised when transport is inaccessible (MacConville 2007).

KNOWLEDGE AND UNDERSTANDING

Children and young people with disabilities and/or special educational needs may perceive that there is limited knowledge and understanding of their individual needs among teachers. For example, despite parental support one young person with dyslexia encountered little appreciation of her difficulties:

> At primary level mum picked up that I had a problem in high infants and when she went she was told that she was just being an over concerned parent and that I just had a lack of concentration and I was lazy so all the way through I was told that even when I was diagnosed I had a certain teacher that had a huge problem with me going for extra classes and he told me that I was stupid and I was just slow and that I would want to stop using it as an excuse. (Kenny *et al.* 2000, p.32)

From the same study, there sometimes appeared to be a fundamental lack of basic knowledge about the impact of disabling conditions/special educational needs on student participation, and some teachers demonstrated a lack of awareness through their interactions:

> It can come across in the way they speak to you – they might speak slower which is really annoying. (p.45)

> There were some of the old teachers if you asked them to repeat they'd think you were taking the p… to be exact and they'd start giving out to you and everything it was so annoying. (p.30)

There also appeared sometimes to be confusion over dyslexia:

> I think I understand with me there's a novelty oh she just can't read there's very little known about dyslexia out there. I think that's why people get the wrong idea for me. I have no sounds for the letters but that is the last thing people think of when it comes to dyslexia you read backwards, I have no short term memory either which is another thing so you have to educate people and you have to let them know. (unpublished transcript)

Children with ASDs can frequently be misunderstood by adults and teachers, with their behaviour being characterized as rude, naughty and difficult, when in fact the child in question may not have understood the context for the interaction and from the adult perspective have acted inappropriately (MacConville 2007).

SCHOOL CLASSROOM ENVIRONMENT

In some school settings parents/carers may perceive that their children are under pressure to conform to school expectations, even though their disability might make this extremely difficult. In one case a school arranged a meeting with parents to reassure them that the participation of a particular child would not be detrimental to the other children in the class. Other parents have reported that their child appears to be constantly singled out as different because of their disability. There is also a perception that children with visible disabilities are more appropriately catered for compared to children with learning and/or behavioural difficulties.

In examining school experiences from the perspective of pupils with dyslexia, it has been found that they often feel frustrated and anxious if their difficulties are not sensitively handled, and that often they are characterized as lazy and/or lacking concentration. Pupils have recounted the negative impact of public failure in reading and spelling for their self-esteem and their motivation for learning (MacConville 2007). The classroom becomes a particularly hostile place for these children when their private difficulties in learning are publicly exposed to their classmates often triggering embarrassment, shame and bullying. Similar perceptions and experiences are apparent in the following, where a pupil recognizes the hidden subtext in classroom interactions:

> I wouldn't ask for help. You might not be actually told you're stupid, but you're getting the hidden messages so you're not going to go 'I'm stupid can I have help?' Like writing down homework from the blackboard was a nightmare for me – I always went home with half sentences or with the same sentence down three times. (Kenny *et al.* 2000, p.25)

From the same study, there appeared to be a lack of understanding of the effort expended on homework by a student with dyslexia:

> In primary school you were talking 3/4 hours home work. Mum would go and say look she's 9 years of age I will give her an hour and whatever she doesn't gets done in the hour but that was fine to mums face but when the when you were in class it was a different story. (pp.32–33)

PEER RELATIONSHIPS

As mentioned earlier over-reliance on peer support to address basic access needs can have a negative effect on peer relationships for children with disabilities and/or special educational needs. Interactions between children with and without disabilities may often be dominated by a discourse of need and care, and as a result 'the non-disabled children behaved not as equals, but as guides or helpers' (Watson *et al.* 1999, p.17).

The labels routinely assigned to children, such as dyslexia and autism, can be subject to misinterpretation by the peer group who lack knowledge about these conditions. These children can be characterized as 'thick' by their peers and this negative perception can have a profound impact on their lives (MacConville 2007).

Misunderstandings about the nature of disability/special educational need can affect interactions:

> Sometimes some of the students can get the idea that if you have a physical disability you also have a mental disability and so that can work hand in hand and people beside you are getting A's and B's and I'm bordering getting a D and that great for me to be quite honest and its hard for them to understand then and I suppose in a sense you really know who your friends are they stick by you the best to be quite honest and am they understand they take the time to listen they understand there is nothing wrong with you but am there a few people who consider that if you have a physical you have a mental disability you just try to ignore them. (Kenny *et al.* 2000, Unpublished transcript)

Another student in this study had experienced school from both the non-disabled and the disabled perspective as she had a life-threatening illness and as a result had impaired mobility. She discovered that her peers lacked basic knowledge of her condition:

> A lad in my class said 'being sick wouldn't have anything to do with your brain' and I said I think it might. He didn't realise what is wrong with me, which is hard to cope with in some ways. I feel I have to put it out in the open when I see people. (p.40)

She also observed that lack of awareness could have negative results:

> It was unreal the slagging (verbal insults) and it can be at disabled people. They're just doing it for a joke; they don't know what the person feels. (p.40)

DEVELOPING AUTONOMY

Developing autonomy is evidently a critical feature in the maturation process for all children. However, establishing an appropriate level of independence in social interactions and in learning is not always a straightforward process.

Some of the barriers to establishing autonomy can be directly attributable to how schools conceptualize and implement support relationships for children and young people. 'Helping' relationships by their very nature are complex, and we cannot uncritically assume that this type of support is unproblematic for the young people involved. Serious reservations about these 'helping' relationships have been expressed by young people in a number of studies (Horgan 2003; Wilson and Jade 1999). Often these difficulties emerge in the relationship with the special needs assistant.

Receiving help from special needs assistants made one child feel different from his classmates, though he responded by characterizing these support people as his 'bodyguards' thus attempting to change peer perception about why he was receiving their support (Curtin and Clarke 2005). Young people can feel very vulnerable in this situation, as they have to communicate their most intimate needs, sometimes to a person of the opposite sex. As a result, the young people often feel that their privacy is compromised; that they are disempowered and have little control over their lives. Over-protective 'mothering' from well-meaning assistants can be particularly frustrating, especially when basic access issues are involved (MacConville 2007).

The struggle for recognition, autonomy and access to the curriculum can impose a significant personal cost for the young person involved. One young person with dyslexia withdrew from peer interaction and experienced a serious loss of confidence in herself as a person:

> I didn't get involved at all in anything because I was always trying to survive get through school I suppose confidence wise I just dropped because of the general attitude I went into a world of my own and I didn't bother. I couldn't mix with people I couldn't I didn't have the ability – confidence was a huge thing I had none I had none. I suppose I excluded myself I didn't feel that I was worth anything again it comes back to the confidence I wasn't the type of child that would burst into a room bubbly I was just too caught up in I hated school I hated everything about it I spent my whole life trying to be sick you know the earaches and stomach aches that was me and I think that why mum knew there was such a big problem because I hated school so much is I just went in and tired to survive the day I wasn't bullied

or picked on I just I know I just switched off for an awful lot of years. (Kenny *et al.* 2000, unpublished transcript)

Case study 2.1 David: giving a voice to an excluded pupil

During his early years, David attended his local Montessori school. This segued into a brief attendance at his local mainstream primary. David was a quiet young child who slept well but resisted interacting, preferring instead his own company. While David was slow to reach his developmental milestones he didn't have a diagnosis of Asperger syndrome until he was eight years old. This prompted a move to a special class in another mainstream school.

While David experienced some success in primary school he presented with nuanced variations of the triad of impairments (in the domains of social interaction, communication and imagination), not to mention preoccupation with special interests associated with narrow, repetitive patterns of activities and resistance to change. While David was a good communicator he did not understand everything you said. It was important to check that he had understood. While he communicated extensively about his hobbies and interests, long periods of reciprocal communication tired him.

Initiating friendships was difficult for him and he struggled with social ineptness and awkwardness and liked to retreat to the safety of his familiar patterns of response, avoiding the challenges of the social world. His social difficulties led to bullying and isolation within the primary school and inadvertently led to frayed teacher–student relations. David's difficulties within the classroom were exacerbated as his work pattern and performance was uneven and teaching strategies that appeared to work one day were not necessarily successful the following day.

While his parents attended Individual Education Plan meetings and were involved in decisions regarding curriculum, attendance at soccer practice and art class with mainstream students, behaviour difficulties began to emerge during these years. David's behaviours became more intense – more challenging for the school, less manageable, and more measurable. Contrasting images of David revealed a boy lost in the creative world of art – quiet, peaceful, joyfully immersed; or a boy with sensory and coordination difficulties, struggling with competitive games, a slowly ebbing self-esteem, and no friends.

David was moved school. It was decided that a more effective environment to accommodate his behaviours was needed. David's behaviours needed to be contained. Multi-disciplinary investigations revealed evidence of increasing levels of anxiety and depression and spiralling displays of aggression. David was now excluded from public places. School trips were no longer a viable option as he was excluded from the public transport necessary to get there.

David at 14 had reached the end of his participation in the formal education system and was enrolled in a programme that attempted to cater for young people who for whatever reason had been excluded from school. I was engaged as a teacher to support David's learning within this setting. In an initial discussion with David's parents it was apparent that David particularly enjoyed an art class where classroom walls and windows provided a canvas for his expression. Dynamic consultations ensued; we asked David what he liked doing, what he was good at, where his talents lay and what he found difficult. We explored how we could incorporate these into his programme. We tried to accommodate difficulties and embed a sense of achievement, noting our successes and failures.

It was important to explore ways that he could be empowered and encouraged to participate in the design of his own learning goals. This took many forms, but was mainly through the media of his specific skills and interests. We usually approached the curriculum by breaking down larger concepts into more achievable short-term goals, using the media preferred by David. We sometimes relied on his excellent memory and frequently worked by discussing David's fascination with dates and numbers and used his amazing visual recall in the development of dialogue around learning outcomes.

Combining words, feelings and visual images was difficult for David, but his participation was stimulated if he saw that his opinions began to count or if his suggestions were taken on board. This also worked effectively if David was given some choice around how he wanted to behave, but at the same time exploring the parameters of acceptable behaviour and performing picture and role rehearsal of situations that were challenging. It was important to account for David's difficulty with generalized learning as well as difficulties with incidental learning; skills needed to be taught consistently in many contexts and with several people. Further support for David's organizational difficulties embedded a sense of structure, routine, predictability and systematic planning in his everyday school life.

Of course there were situations where David found it very hard to express himself; this usually concerned interpersonal relations and social interaction. We used several social and emotional literacy skills strategies to combat these difficulties, including ultimately a buddy system.

However, as a prerequisite to implementing the buddy system, I felt that it was important to have already engendered a feeling of David's value and worth in the classroom, not just acceptance or over-reliance on his factual knowledge. As a precursor to engaging socially with groups of students, David needed explicit instruction in areas such as listening, attending, conversing, interpreting social cues and the intricacies of meta-language.

Work on communication focused on speech and drama activities, explicit teaching of conversational pragmatics and the use of drama and social stories. Video recording of role-played scenarios highlighted contrasting themes; anger versus calm, requesting versus demanding, etc. Commentary was invited after viewing, enhancing the power of reflection. David also needed to develop an awareness of perspectives and empathy; occasionally we worked on attitudes, respect, responsibility and demonstration of affect towards others.

While self-confidence and self-efficacy were key target areas, I encouraged the use of poetry and biographical work to connect thought to feeling and to promote some level of self-disclosure. Interpretation of concrete imagery, simile and metaphor were tied to attempts at narrative. Capturing poetic and sensory images on canvas provided concrete evidence of David's ability to think in pictures and became tools to explore internal processes, theory of mind and emotional literacy. Our journey towards autobiographical expression was challenging. It wasn't that David didn't have feelings, it's that he didn't know how to express them. Work towards developing interpersonal and intrapersonal attributes was designed to assist in his social and lifelong development.

It was essential to provide a predictable and safe environment; minimising transitions, planning and rehearsing when change was unavoidable. We offered David a consistent daily routine: trying to foresee changes and using written or visual schedules and timetables accordingly. Sensory difficulties were impacting on David's ability to cope with the world around him. The degree of difficulty varied from one day to another. Most frequently, David perceived ordinary sensations as intense, but he was occasionally under-reactive to certain stimuli. David's sensory and motor issues added to his difficulties with social interaction. David needed individual attention and opportunities to work on and practise motor skills necessary for developing more coordinated movements associated with organized sports. David also needed the option of avoiding these.

A sensitive approach towards the treatment of isolated pursuits was needed. This was worked on by allowing specific time periods for engagement in these pursuits. In the case of art, assignments were given that allowed full exploration of David's talents. In the case of more challenging subjects (e.g. English), David was encouraged to blend art and literature in his approach to areas such as creative writing. Incorporation of abilities, talents and obsessive interests as a bridge to his existing educational programme was initially demanding – our path rarely wandered from them. Occasionally, obsessive interests with one aspect of a subject, particularly history, could interfere with learning the next concept. This strategy needed to be applied and monitored with caution; a project-based approach usually worked well in an attempt to connect and broaden knowledge and learning across other subject areas. If obsessive interests became dominant, a more structured approach was used – David was assigned specific topics which would provide a springboard to the actual assignment. Aspects of the TEACCH approach 'work then play', or a 'least to most' approach, were quite successful. The capacity to enjoy learning opportunities and to expand David's existing interests was something we devoted much time to.

In terms of voice, David experienced difficulty modulating his and had a tendency to speak too softly. In terms of its prosodic features, there were unusual rhythms, cadences and inflections; however, David did not show reticence when complaining or insisting on his ideas. Pragmatic and paralinguistic features – impulsive outbursts or blunt personal statements – occasionally appeared rude, arrogant or gauche.

An inability to understand idioms, sarcasm, jokes or irony did not endear David to the group. David's difficulties with interpreting facial expressions and body language added to these problems and hindered his ability to speak confidently. Accepting and enjoying his literalness of understanding and meaning was a challenge, but also a key to relating to David. Accommodation of language idiosyncrasies allowed a better view of David's world. David's need for clear, literal and unambiguous requests and instructions were met with easy translation and better understanding.

Reading aloud also raised difficulties. Individual work, or work with a buddy or small supportive group, provided opportunities for practice, and slowly this valuable skill began to emerge as inhibitions and obstacles faded. A successful alternative form of communication was the use of a laptop. David was computer literate and enjoyed this as a form of presentation for his ideas.

Providing David with a forum for his participation allowed us to gain better insight into how to support him and what he needed to build more positive relationships with the learning material, teachers and fellow students. It also allowed for a co-construction of learning and, remarkably, a reflection on the process itself.

Any student's ability to locate and find their voice is challenging during the adolescent years. David sometimes found it difficult to accept his diagnosis and our interpretation of it. Occasionally he was not comfortable with the effects of his condition, and this interfered with factors relating to his ability and life experience. Low self-esteem, depression and anxiety pervaded the dark days. They were debilitating and isolating, emphasizing the need to make his environment less disabling and to focus on his strengths, abilities and refreshing difference.

After building secure foundations in the areas of social and communicative competence, it became important to teach David the skills to advocate for himself across a variety of settings. The outcome of all of these aspects of competence was measured by his ability to increase his social and communication skills and interactions. In this regard, David was better able to formulate new relationships and demonstrate reciprocal communication with unfamiliar people.

REFLECTING ON DAVID'S STORY

In giving David's story further thought, a number of salient insights emerge. It is apparent that difficulties were consistently traced back to David's diagnosis, his refusal to cooperate, communication differences and lack of appropriate social skills. David was being described by what he couldn't do, how he didn't fit in and how he didn't belong or connect with his peers or environment.

His difficulties with change were further compounded by poorly planned transitions, and lack of collaboration, which failed to consider how David would be affected by these changes. Engaging, connecting and working with David required work on developing a repertoire of meaningful interactions and communication strategies. Vulnerability to changing stimuli required careful readjustment, repair and encouragement of self-regulation when environments are threatening and combative, or circumstances change.

David needed to learn new ways to override the maladaptive strategies. He needed to know that his world was safe and that discontinuities became connected. Schools can learn from the type of personalized intervention described here, where David was centrally involved in devising strategies to support his learning.

Recognizing and responding to needs

While this chapter, and in particular Case study 2.1, has focused on the barriers to participation experienced by children and young people with special educational needs, there is evidence that schools need to be aware that all children can experience marginalization. Supportive peer relationships are critical to the personal and emotional development of all children, yet unless there is a positive emotional climate within the classroom, children will not thrive. Opportunities for bullying may be inadvertently created and classrooms can become hostile places. Case study 2.1 effectively illustrates the necessity for schools and teachers to work to the child's strengths and avoid labelling children unnecessarily. Recognizing what all children can offer to the classroom life because of their diversity can be a useful first step in responding appropriately to the real needs of all children to belong and learn together in a supportive classroom atmosphere.

SUMMARY

In this chapter we have:

- explored the types of barriers that inhibit the participation of pupils with special educational needs in school
- outlined how access issues can compromise the involvement of pupils with special educational needs within the classroom
- considered how inappropriate teacher assumptions and expectations can have a negative influence on the attempts of pupils with special educational needs to make progress in their learning
- examined how the lack of a supportive learning environment can create difficulties in fostering autonomy and positive peer relationships for pupils with special educational needs
- seen how what we learn from children and young people with disabilities and/or special educational needs can inform the way classrooms can be run for the benefit of all.

REFERENCES

Curtin, M. and Clarke, G. (2005) 'Listening to young people with physical disabilities' experiences of education.' *International Journal of Disability, Development and Education 52*, 3, 195–214.

Horgan, G. (2003) 'Educable: Disabled Young People in Northern Ireland Challenge the Education System.' In M. Shevlin and R. Rose (eds) *Encouraging Voices: Respecting the Insights of Young People Who Have Been Marginalised* (pp.100–120). Dublin: National Disability Authority.

Kenny, M., McNeela, E., Shevlin, M. and Daly, T. (2000) *Hidden Voices: Young People with Disabilities Speak about Their Second Level Schooling.* Cork: South West Regional Authority.

Kenny, M., McNeela, E., Noonan Walsh, P. and Shevlin, M. (2003) *'In The Morning – The Dark Opens'. A Study of the Experience of Parents of Children with Down Syndrome and Other Learning Disabilities in Mainstream Schools: Why This Choice Was Made, How It Was Achieved and Hopes for the Future.* Dublin: Centre for Disability Studies, University College Dublin and National Institute for Intellectual Disability, Trinity College Dublin. (Funded by UNESCO.)

McArthur, J., Sharp, S., Kelly, B. and Gaffney, M. (2007) 'Disabled children negotiating school life: agency, difference and teaching practice.' *International Journal of Children's Rights 15*, 1–22.

MacConville, R. (2007) *Looking at Inclusion: Listening to the Voices of Young People.* London: Paul Chapman.

Priestley, M. (2001) 'Introduction: The Global Context of Disability.' In M. Priestley (ed. *Disability and the Life Course: Global Perspectives* (pp.3–14). Cambridge: Cambridge University Press.

Watson, N., Shakespeare, T., Cunningham-Burley, S., Barnes, C., Corker, M., Davis, J. and Priestley, M. (1999) *Life as a Disabled Child: A Qualitative Study of Young People's Experiences and Perspectives. Final Report.* Swindon: Economic and Social Research Council.

Wilson, C. and Jade, R. (1999) *Whose Voice Is It Anyway? Talking to Disabled Young People at School.* London: Alliance for Inclusive Education.

CHAPTER 3

Helping Students to Participate in Their Learning

Within this chapter we will explore how children and young people, and particularly those with special educational needs, can be encouraged to become active participants in their classroom learning. This will entail an examination of current practice in relation to teacher–pupil discussion around learning, an elucidation of the potential for development and a consideration of the existing barriers. We will focus on enabling pupils to engage with their learning processes; developing a positive identity as a learner; and creating the appropriate environment for a discussion of teaching and learning between teachers and pupils.

While teaching and learning processes are evidently central to classroom life there appears to be remarkably little discussion between teachers and pupils about what is actually involved in these processes. As a result, teaching and learning discourse can be very minimalist and focus on attainment and performance in a very narrow sense. However, when pupils are active participants in discussing their own learning there is considerable evidence that they are capable of discussing their learning in a very balanced perceptive manner (Reay 2006).

To an increasing extent official policy documents have addressed teaching and learning issues with an emphasis on the desirability of enhancing the role of pupil consultation and participation. For example, the Scottish Curriculum for Excellence (2004) recommends that pupil consultation should infuse all aspects of school and classroom practice and not be confined to individual teachers and/or school committees (Deuchar 2009).

The expanded guidance to the Special Educational Needs Code of Practice (2001) emphasizes the role of pupils in participating in decision-making processes around their learning and school experiences.

> For the first time, children and young people with special needs are being actively encouraged by education policy to be involved in planning what services they receive at school and in communicating their views on how they should be delivered. (Klein 2003, p.42)

The Code of Practice recommends that:

> where possible, they [children and young people with special educational needs] should participate in all the decision-making processes that occur in education including the setting of learning targets and contributing to IEPs, discussion about choice of schools, contributing to the assessment of their needs and to the annual review and transition process.

The Code of Practice recognizes that realizing this in practice can be fraught with problems and quite difficult dilemmas to resolve. Teachers and support staff will have to make judgements about the level of participation appropriate for particular children and young people. As the Code points out:

> ...there is a fine balance between giving the child a voice and encouraging them to make informed decisions and overburdening them with decision-making procedures where they have insufficient experience and knowledge to make appropriate judgements without additional support.

While pupil participation is explicitly mentioned in the Code of Practice, this participation is predicated on professional intervention that involves practitioners determining, managing and representing pupil views rather than empowering the pupils themselves to become active participants in the decision-making processes that affect their lives (May 2005).

Often, official policies appear to favour pupil involvement in particular activities, such as individual education planning, rather than endorsing the concept of pupil involvement in all aspects of school life. This view is in marked contrast to a number of European initiatives that actively promote pupil involvement in crucial areas of school life (Deuchar 2009; Klein 2003) as outlined in the Euridem Project (reviewed by Davies and Kilpatrick 2000). For example, in Denmark 'teaching and learning takes place within a dialogue culture, in which discussions are a major part of class time' (Klein 2003, p.21). In Swedish schools democratic structures are the norm and schools aim to enable pupils to take responsibility for their work and to play a dynamic part in influencing their learning.

BARRIERS TO CONSULTATION ABOUT TEACHING AND LEARNING

Facilitating pupil consultation is complex and challenging for schools, teachers, pupils, professionals and policy makers. We perhaps need to make a distinction between obtaining pupil perspectives/choices and involving pupils in shared decision making (Norwich and Kelly 2006). Eliciting pupil preferences can be relatively straightforward compared to the negotiating process involved in shared decision making.

Barriers to consultation with pupils about teaching and learning exist at many levels including systemic, school policy, teacher attitudes and pupil reactions to consultation. Within the UK context the dominance of the standards and attainment agenda often precludes the pursuit of meaningful consultation with pupils about teaching and learning. There is a persistent belief among teachers that pupil participation constitutes an ordinary aspect of classroom life and that this type of participation constitutes consultation with pupils. Ordinary classroom teaching does involve significant consultation with pupils, but this is rarely about teaching and learning (Rudduck and McIntyre 2007). While informal consultations are valuable, effective consultation requires a more strategic approach that makes the consultation process explicit to pupils and teachers (Rudduck and McIntyre 2007). Professionals can believe that pupils, because of their age and/or limited cognitive ability, are too immature to participate meaningfully in decision making around their classroom learning. But it has been pointed out that children's right to express a view is dependent only on their capacity to form a view, whether this view is mature or not is irrelevant to the core principle (Lundy 2007).

Consultation with pupils/young people can be undermined if there is any indication of tokenism (Woolfson et al. 2008). Unsatisfactory consultations have also been reported when the young people were not able to express their views satisfactorily or felt that their views had not been adequately acknowledged. Some pupils believe their participation in decision-making processes is limited by the fact that they have no control over how professionals represent their views (Norwich and Kelly 2006). Pupils also mention other limiting factors, including problems in establishing trusting relationships on which to build genuine partnerships, unapproachable teachers and the reality that positive outcomes from the participation process are not always visible in the short term (Norwich and Kelly 2006). Pupils may not be used to having their views taken seriously by adults; as a result implementing appropriate pupil consultation about learning will have to overcome this initial scepticism about the value of the exercise (Deuchar 2009).

BENEFITS OF CONSULTATION

There is evidence that consulting pupils can have positive outcomes in a number of domains (Rudduck and McIntyre 2007):

- a stronger sense of membership, feeling more positive about school and more included in its purposes – the organizational dimension
- a stronger sense of respect and self-worth so that they feel positive about themselves – the personal dimension
- a stronger sense of self-as-learner so that they are better able to manage their own learning – the pedagogic dimension
- a stronger sense of agency so that they see it as worthwhile to contribute to improvement in teaching and learning and wider school matters – the political dimension.

Engaging in consulting pupils about teaching and learning can be risky, as the usual patterns of classroom interaction are challenged. Customary roles and expectations are confronted and the power relationship between teacher and pupils subtly redefined. But both teachers and pupils stand to benefit from this type of consultation process focused on teaching and learning (Rudduck and McIntyre 2007).

Teachers can learn from their pupils what is working well within the classroom and how learning process can be made more meaningful and effective. Through consultation pupils can begin to understand their own learning better and develop confidence in their ability to take greater responsibility for their learning and recognize their contribution to improving the conditions for learning within the classroom.

Engaging in learning-focused dialogue is helpful in identifying learning difficulties and can also enable pupils to reflect on and improve their learning. Potential benefits for pupils from this type of dialogue include (Flutter and Rudduck 2004):

- an understanding of learning processes
- the acquisition of a practical language for discussing learning

- an opportunity to develop higher order thinking skills
- increased self-confidence.

In a consultation about learning with younger pupils who have special educational needs the children appeared to gain in confidence, were more motivated and became more active participants in the school community (Jelly, Fuller and Byers 2000).

It has been observed that teachers can learn about the learning processes by engaging with the less proficient learners in their classrooms (Rudduck and McIntyre 2007). These are often the children and young people who are reluctant to talk about their learning processes and perhaps have had negative experiences of schooling. Yet the perspectives of these less accomplished learners can provide valuable insights into the causal factors in difficulties in learning experienced.

In the majority of cases these difficulties in learning are overcome, and the children and young people can emerge with an enhanced set of strategies to address future difficulties (Flutter and Rudduck 2004). However, for a significant minority these difficulties persist and become an entrenched feature of their classroom experiences. Young learners are particularly fearful of 'falling behind' their peers in learning. This experience can motivate some children to make greater effort, but it can have the opposite effect on others who can opt out of the challenge and engage in inappropriate behaviour to avoid being 'found out'. All children can experience some difficulty in learning at some stage of their educational career. Pupils themselves have outlined the key areas (Flutter and Rudduck 2004):

- a question of time
- understanding assessment
- understanding the criteria for 'good' work
- the impact of friendships on learning
- sustaining pupils' engagement with learning
- building a positive identity as a learner.

While these difficulties apply to varying degrees to all learners it is very evident that children and young people with special educational needs experience persistent problems in all the key areas outlined. Within the remainder of this chapter we will focus on three critical areas: sustaining pupils' engagement with learning; building a positive identity as a learner; and creating a supportive environment for teacher–pupil discourse on learning.

ENGAGING PUPILS IN LEARNING

While teachers set targets in order to help pupils improve the quality of their learning this is often not apparent to the pupils who feel overwhelmed by the demands without the necessary support. Pupils report that there is often little or no discussion of the target with the pupil or any indication of how the pupil might acquire the strategies required to address the learning target. In effect what should be an effective educational strategy to support pupil learning can become, in the absence of appropriate teacher–pupil discussion, another obstacle to learning that the pupil is expected to overcome (Flutter and Rudduck 2004).

In an examination of the process of encouraging children to contribute to learning plans, positive outcomes were reported when genuine pupil consultation took place. The study suggested that the best way to motivate pupils to improve their learning involves engaging them at the beginning and ensuring that their views are included in the planning process (Morton 1996). In this study children chose a range of targets, some physical, others about acquiring particular knowledge and specific skills. Children were steered through the target-setting process and encouraged to choose two targets, one easier and the other harder. The children then identified the type of support required to achieve their chosen target and were asked to say how they will know when they have reached their target. Enabling pupils to make real choices about learning targets and acquiring a sense of ownership appear to be the critical factors in more highly motivated and committed pupils.

Another study revealed some disquieting facts about the lack of pupil knowledge about their own Individual Education Plans (Lovitt, Plavins and Cushing 1999). Half of the pupils ($N=162$) reported that they had a sketchy idea of what an Individual Education Plan (IEP) consisted of, an equal number had participated in an IEP meeting in the previous year and 23 pupils were able to describe an IEP goal from their learning plan. These pupil reports would suggest that often the individual education planning process did not involve even the most basic levels of participation from the pupils concerned. One pupil reported that the IEP remained broadly similar even as his educational career progressed:

> Well I think it really is pretty stupid. I do my work and everything in school. I did everything that was on the list. But each year there is always an IEP. And each year the objectives are exactly the same… Just basically learning the same stuff over and over and over every year. And it's been like that since about 8th grade. (Lovitt *et al.* 1999, p.71)

Teachers can help pupils to learn and achieve their learning goals through carefully explaining the purpose of the task and giving a concrete demonstration as one pupil observed:

> If you tell me the purpose, like in a car, this is what this is, this is what it does, and this is why it works that way. Then I can, you know, zoom right past it. If you don't do that and you go, here are the instructions, go ahead I will be lost. I get real lost real easy. I have to have somebody helping me through. (Lovitt *et al.*, 1999, p.72)

POSITIVE IDENTITY AS A LEARNER

Developing a positive identity as a learner can be a challenging task for all learners, though for pupils with special educational needs there can be considerable obstacles to overcome. Pupils with special educational needs often struggle with negative perceptions of their abilities and capacities as learners.

External factors such as low achievement in assessments tend to reinforce these negative sentiments, and pupil self-perception as a deficit learner can become firmly embedded. It is apparent that lower-achieving pupils welcome the opportunity to discuss their learning with a teacher and/or parent (Flutter and Rudduck 2004). Reflecting on learning and focusing on achievements in learning as well as difficulties can help these pupils to regain some confidence in learning.

Pupils generally prefer these discussions in private on a one-to-one basis. Facilitating the development of a positive identity as a learner with and for pupils with special educational needs can encounter difficulties in teacher attitudes and the perception of pupils of themselves as learners. For example, teachers may not believe that lower-achieving pupils who routinely disengage from learning have anything worthwhile to say about the learning process. It may be very difficult:

> to disentangle the mutually reinforcing tendencies for the less successful pupils to have less expected of them by their teachers and therefore be less motivated to engage with school learning, less enthusiastic about being able to comment on it and less confident that if they do express a view that anyone will take any notice of what they have to say. (Rudduck and McIntyre 2007, p.159)

It is difficult for both teachers and pupils to extricate themselves from this downward spiral when pupil reticence to contribute to the discussion on learning can be interpreted as not caring rather than the consequence of pupil disengagement as a result of persistent failure in learning. Teachers can be surprised at the depth of insight into learning offered by the disengaged pupils; and these are the very pupils that teachers need to hear from in order to change the negative dynamic of existing teacher and pupil perspectives on learning and ascertain whether 'the respect, recognition and trust that are fundamental to consultation could help restore their [pupils'] belief in schooling' (Rudduck and McIntyre 2007, p.160).

There is often a risk that teachers can be over-protective of pupils who have disabilities and/or special educational needs (Bjarnason 2004). This type of paternalism, while well intentioned, can result in teachers emphasizing the affective aspect of the learning environment to the detriment of extending pupil learning. Pupils feeling good about themselves and being occupied can be worthwhile objectives but not at the expense of the pupil being insufficiently challenged and their potential for learning seriously underestimated. Reducing social isolation is another valuable objective and may be a necessary precondition for learning but should not become a substitute or alternative to meaningful engagement in the process of academic learning.

In one study, teachers were reported by pupils to be practising avoidance strategies by not including them in ordinary classroom interactions and opportunities for learning (Bjarnason 2004):

> Sometimes a teacher avoids asking me questions, skip over me when students are asked to read something. (p.197)

> You were not really allowed to try out new things and get burnt. (p.168)

One pupil was particularly frustrated when a teacher excused him from reading:

> In a recent lesson the teacher said to me: 'I will not let you read now because you are tired.' They don't really understand that one does not want to be spared. The teacher should make exactly the same demands on all. (p.197)

Another pupil who is deaf considered that teachers had, for whatever reason, been unable to communicate in any meaningful way with him:

> It was as if I was behind a curtain, nobody had the courage to talk to me. (p.173)

Children and young people who have disabilities often encounter many threats to their identity that make acquiring a positive identity as a learner more problematic. Pupils in another study reported difficulties in retaining a modicum of privacy as their medical conditions were openly discussed in front of their peers (Watson *et al.* 1999). Obviously this seriously disadvantaged these pupils in their quest for a positive identity as a young person before there is even a consideration of developing a constructive identity as a learner.

Disabled children are able to make teachers aware of how their learning could be enhanced in the classroom. For example, in a study of disabled schoolchildren one child pointed out that withdrawal for extra reading support was ineffective as he was expected to complete the class work he had missed. One teacher responded to this situation by endeavouring to incorporate the supplementary reading for disabled children into the class programme. Another teacher demonstrated a capacity to make adjustments to classroom arrangements to support the learning of disabled children. This child disliked the constant presence of the teacher aide, and the teacher assigned the teacher aide the role of more general support within the classroom thus respecting the wishes of the child (MacArthur *et al.* 2007).

Active participation in class discussions can be problematic where children have speech difficulties, and this situation may require teachers to take creative approaches to encouraging participation; or the children themselves often feel they have to take the lead:

> ...some disabled children had to prove their ability to their peers and teachers, and challenge negative expectations for their learning. Joanne explained: 'just that 'cos some people think that being disabled is the worst thing ever, but I just like proving people wrong like 'cos some people say 'Oh you can't do that' and then I show them that I can. And just showing people that I can do – I can try to do everything. (MacArthur *et al.* 2007, p.10)

Teachers face the difficult challenge of responding appropriately to children's impairment-related differences while not emphasizing the differences between these children and their peers: 'There is a fine line between denying or minimising disabled children's learning, behaviour, communication or physical challenges on the one hand, and highlighting difference on the other' (MacArthur et al. 2007, p.16).

An appreciation of diversity is highlighted as a critical component in fostering active pupil participation in learning:

This approach deconstructs difference and rejects the notion of a 'normal' group of children, encouraging teachers to adopt pedagogical practices that enable diverse groups of children to work together as caring, cohesive and inclusive learning communities. Learning is fundamentally conceptualised as taking place within the social context of relationships with teachers and peers. (Higgins, MacArthur and Kelly, 2009, pp.480-481)

Improved pedagogy and supportive social relationships can significantly modify negative perceptions of difference and impairment.

It has been observed that lower-achieving pupils learn to be greatly reliant on the opinion of others about their capacity to complete learning tasks in direct contrast to more able pupils who take greater responsibility for their own learning (Arnot and Reay 2004). This 'learned helplessness' of lower-achieving pupils could affect both their willingness to persist with learning tasks and their ability to evaluate their own learning. Lower-achieving pupils believe that they have little if any control over their own learning (Rudduck and McIntyre 2007). Any learning that occurs is attributed to additional teacher support rather than pupil effort and ability.

These pupils may often find the work set too easy and unchallenging (e.g. worksheets); however, they can be fearful that if this became apparent to the teacher then the work could become too difficult to complete (Rudduck and McIntyre 2007). The social dynamic of the classroom sometimes makes it very difficult for lower-achieving pupils to admit their difficulties in learning as they would be embarrassed among their peers and could be ridiculed.

Often pupils resolve this situation by resisting teacher efforts to persuade them to work and by adopting a nonchalant approach to learning. Also these pupils may attempt to assert some control over their learning environment through disruptive behaviour that seizes teacher attention but also has a negative impact on pupil learning.

CREATING A SUPPORTIVE ENVIRONMENT FOR PARTICIPATION

The principle of participation applies to all children including those who have special educational needs. In attempting to implement this principle, schools tend to develop school-specific approaches. A useful distinction can be drawn between formal and informal participation by children and young people in school life (Norwich and Kelly 2006). Formal participation tends to entail specific procedures for defined purposes and for children and young people with special educational needs this usually involves a legally mandated identification and assessment process. Conversely, informal participation refers to everyday interactions where children's views are listened to and respected. As one head teacher put it, the informal and formal processes are inextricably linked and interdependent:

> ...it is about being polite to children and walking down the corridor and saying hello to them. Little things like this make a big difference as they feel safe and secure. Then you put in the more specific things like peer mediators and IEPs. (Norwich and Kelly 2006, p.261)

Guaranteeing pupil participation in the formal statutory processes appears to be predicated on whether general daily participative practices are firmly established in school life. Deeply embedded participatory school practice has usually been found to result in school staff finding ways meaningfully to include children with special educational needs in statutory IEP and statementing processes.

Children and young people with additional support needs can be adamant that they should be actively involved in all aspects of managing their additional learning needs, including identification, assessment and review (Woolfson *et al.* 2008). These pupils recognize that the statutory assessment processes have serious implications not only for their current school careers but also for their future as learners and later as adults.

Active participation for these pupils involves being fully cognisant of discussions about their learning needs, having a say in who participated in these discussions and providing a significant input into the outcomes of these deliberations. Involving children with special educational needs in assessment, planning and review processes can have significant benefits, such as encouraging increased motivation, autonomy, knowledge of learning styles, awareness of strengths and difficulties in learning and enabling the children to take greater responsibility for their own progress in learning (Roller 1998).

It has been found that pupil participation in contributing to the statutory assessment processes and developing and reviewing IEPs varies significantly between schools (Norwich and Kelly 2006). In some schools pupils participate in every aspect of the IEP process, in others limited consultation is apparent due to the IEP workload in the school. Some schools modify the consultation process to take account of the child's age and ability level, resulting in a limited dialogue around specific targets deemed appropriate by the classroom teacher/Special Educational Needs Coordinator (SENCO). In some cases pupils participate in parent–teacher meetings though other schools adopt a more protective approach believing that it could be damaging for the child to hear negative feedback on their learning. It is evident that not all children with special educational needs are invited to participate in discussions around their learning plans. Even where participatory practice is the norm in the school, children and young people with communication difficulties and/or cognitive impairments may be excluded from participation. Difficulties have also been reported in eliciting the views of very young school-aged children, though a more indirect approach was advocated by one SENCO:

> They should be involved if they're capable of being involved, so there is no way to know what their level of understanding is, especially with this age group [infants]...so we just gauge what they like and don't like by watching what they do and seeing their reactions, so from that point of view they are involved in the decisions that are being made, not directly... (Norwich and Kelly 2006, p.267)

While schools, teachers and pupils appear to grasp the processes involved in meaningful pupil participation in learning plans there appears to be more ambivalence about extending the concept of participation to include shared decision making and power sharing within aspects of classroom learning.

Active pupil participation in statutory SEN procedures is perceived to be beneficial in facilitating improved learning opportunities and outcomes for pupils and producing a more effective school process that would be able to (Norwich and Kelly 2006):

- inform and influence learning targets, teaching strategies and rewards
- indicate the settings in which to support individual pupils
- inform staff attempts to identify the nature of child's concerns and ways of resolving problems/issues
- give weight to SENCO requests for further learning support
- advise about examination arrangements
- inform the agenda for meetings between parents, teachers and/or other support agencies.

Mentoring has been adopted by a number of schools to address the negative self-perceptions of pupils with special educational needs in relation to learning. Pupil acknowledgement of difficulties in learning can challenge the widespread idea among pupils that it is undesirable to admit any problems with learning. Generally pupils find mentoring a helpful strategy, particularly where it gives targeted support in specific areas of learning:

It's good because in English I get my words muddled up, like Bs and Ds the wrong way round. Ever since I have been with [my mentor] she makes me feel a lot more confident about it. (Year 7 girl cited in Flutter and Rudduck 2004, p.121)

I used to be scared of putting up my hand and saying something and now I am not as scared. (Year 7 boy, cited in Flutter and Ruddick 2004, p.121)

Creating the conditions for sustained engagement with learning and the development of positive identities as learners constituted the core focus within Case study 3.1. While the withdrawal situation described is not necessarily ideal the teacher strove to ensure that this became a positive learning environment and links to mainstream classroom activities were maintained and enhanced.

Case study 3.1 Ms Mangan: building the confidence to achieve

A support teacher, Ms Mangan, worked with a group of six children aged eight to ten years who were withdrawn from the mainstream classroom for intensive support in English and mathematics. Each of these children had encountered serious difficulties in learning including emotional and behavioural difficulties (Clare), emotional difficulties and general learning difficulties (Joanna), dyslexia (Brenda and Ellen) and general learning difficulty (Karen). The group also included a child from the Traveller community who had experienced difficulties in learning, and whose test results placed her in the second and third percentile in English and maths respectively (Carmel).

At the beginning of the year, Ms Mangan decided in order to get to know the children better that each girl should fill in a self-esteem questionnaire (taken from Smith and Call 1999).

This questionnaire explored how the children felt about school, their peers and their learning. Ms Mangan was convinced that while these pupils had a variety of challenges, they were emotionally intelligent and aware of the gaps in their learning. She was also determined that the withdrawal strategy for support that had been recommended by their class teacher was not going to be a negative or diminishing experience for them.

As Ms Mangan read through the questionnaire responses, and compared them with the various test results and psychological reports, there was evidence that the children had responded in a way that was 'appropriate' rather than authentic to themselves, and so this became an area to develop: the opportunity for these pupils to develop their own voice in a way that was non-threatening to them, and that remained within boundaries of age-appropriateness and respect, which were necessary for learning within the school environment.

In English it was decided to focus on the development of good oral language skills, reading and writing, while attempting to improve their (the children's) attitude to learning, and to encourage them to become self-motivated and successful in their work. Each month, the children undertook a writing exercise that would explore their personal likes and dislikes, their dreams and ambitions, or their responses to a variety of challenging situations (Writing Bugs available at http://www.education-world.com/a_lesson/worksheets/index.shtml).

This exercise proved to be a useful writing tool, from many perspectives. The language required to write some of the pieces extended their vocabulary, allowed for opportunities to broaden their understanding of the rules of grammar and punctuation, and permitted them to be creative or realistic, depending on the exercise. In some cases, background knowledge was required, and they learned to use the internet to research appropriately, which also gave an opportunity to introduce basic typing skills and posture.

In reading, the group did not follow the class reader, but instead chose abridged novels (Penguin Readers) that would be within their reading levels but would also be of interest to them. When the children demonstrated that they had grown in confidence about their abilities, the group read one of the novels that their class had read.

In spellings, Ms Mangan encouraged the pupils to set goals and appropriate learning strategies were discussed. The overall strategy was to encourage the pupils to work as a group, helping each other out, and recognizing strengths and needs, so that it became obvious that there was no competition. (One of the pupils had very low self-esteem, and was constantly watching how she was doing in comparison to the others in the group.)

Towards the end of the year, Ms Mangan took one pupil, whose primary difficulty was absenteeism, and who had ability that was thoroughly underdeveloped, in a detailed fashion through the assessment criteria for oral language, reading and writing and gave her time to identify where her ability lay in each area. When she saw her profile of ability in each area, personal targets were set and she requested extra work and time with Ms Mangan in order to improve her profile. Ms Mangan noted that it was important to build up a trusting relationship with the girl and that the girl herself believed in her own ability to improve before embarking on this type of exercise.

There is a growing body of evidence that through encouraging pupils with special educational needs in discussion of their learning profiles positive outcomes occur. Pupils with special educational needs have the capacity to engage with this process and with support can acquire a more positive identity as a learner that can help them overcome difficulties in learning.

Actively engaging in learning

Becoming an active participant in their own learning will benefit all children. Research (Flutter and Rudduck 2004) has clearly indicated that all children benefit from structured consultation about their learning styles and preferences. Constructing classrooms where consultation about learning is encouraged will entail the teacher becoming a facilitator of learning rather than a dispenser of information. All children can gain from taking responsibility for aspects of their learning under the guidance of the teacher. As a result, children and young people actively engage with the learning process and can understand their strengths and difficulties as learners. The pupil reflection exercises on learning described in Case study 3.1 could usefully be replicated in any mainstream classroom with obvious benefits for children's understanding of how to manage their own learning.

SUMMARY

In this chapter we have:

- considered how pupils can become active participants in their own learning
- explored how policy documents recommending increased pupil participation can be actualized
- considered how pupils can be encouraged to maintain and enhance engagement with learning
- examined how supportive environments can be created that enable pupils to develop a positive identity as a learner.

REFERENCES

Arnot, M. and Reay, D. (2004) 'The Social Dynamics of Classroom Learning.' In M. Arnot, D. McIntyre, D. Pedder and D. Reay (eds) *Consultation in the Classroom*. Cambridge: Pearson.

Bjarnason, D. (2004) *New Voices from Iceland: Disability and Young Adulthood*. New York: Nova Science.

Davies, L. and Kilpatrick, G. (2000) *The Euridem Project: A Review of Pupil Democracy in Europe.* London: Children's Rights Alliance for England, Calouste Gulbenkian Foundation, NSPCC.

Deuchar, R. (2009) 'Seen and heard, and then not heard: Scottish pupils' experience of democratic educational practice during the transition from primary to secondary school.' *Oxford Review of Education 35*, 1, 23–40.

Flutter, J. and Rudduck, J. (2004) *Consulting Pupils: What's in It for schools?* Abingdon: Routledge.

Higgins, N., MacArthur, J. and Kelly, B. (2009) 'Including disabled children at school: is it really as simple as "a, c, d"?' *International Journal of Inclusive Education 13*, 5, 471–487.

Jelly, M., Fuller, A. and Byers, R. (2000) *Involving Pupils in Practice: Promoting Partnerships with Pupils with Special Educational Needs.* London: David Fulton Publishers.

Klein, R. (2003) *We Want Our Say: Children as Active Participants in Their Education.* Stoke on Trent: Trentham Books.

Lovitt, T., Plavins, M. and Cushing, S. (1999) 'What do pupils with disabilities have to say about their experience in high school?' *Remedial and Special Education 20*, 67–83.

Lundy, L. (2007) '"Voice" is not enough: conceptualising Article 12 of the United Nations Convention on the Rights of the Child.' *British Educational Research Journal 33*, 6, 927–942.

MacArthur, J., Sharp, S., Kelly, B. and Gaffney, M. (2007) 'Disabled children negotiating school life: agency, difference and teaching practice.' *International Journal of Children's Rights 15*, 1–22.

May, H. (2005) 'Whose participation is it anyway? Examining the context of pupil participation in the UK.' *British Journal of Special Education 32*, 1, 29–34.

Morton, J. (1996) 'Helping children contribute to learning plans.' *Educational and Child Psychology 13*, 2, 23–30.

Norwich, B. and Kelly, N. (2006) 'Evaluating children's participation in SEN procedures: lessons for educational psychologists.' *Educational Psychology in Practice 22*, 3, 255–271.

Reay, D. (2006) '"I'm not seen as one of the clever children": consulting primary school pupils about the social conditions of learning.' *Educational Review 58*, 2, 171–181.

Roller, J. (1998) 'Facilitating pupil involvement in assessment, planning and review processes.' *Educational Psychology in Practice 13*, 4, 266–273.

Rudduck, J. and McIntyre, D. (2007) *Improving Learning through Consulting Pupils.* London: Routledge.

Smith, A. and Call, N. (1999) *The ALPS Approach: Accelerated Learning in Primary Schools.* Stafford: Education Network.

Watson, N., Shakespeare, T., Cunningham-Burley, S., Barnes, C., Corker, M., Davis, J. and Priestley, M. (1999) *Life as a Disabled Child: A Qualitative Study of Young People's Experiences and Perspectives. Final Report.* Swindon: Economic and Social Research Council.

Woolfson, R., Bryce, D., Mooney, L., Harker, M., Lowe, D. and Ferguson, E. (2008) 'Improving methods of consulting with young people: piloting a new model of consultation.' *Educational Psychology in Practice 24*, 1, 55–67.

CHAPTER 4

Principles for Involvement

Teachers who have a commitment to student involvement should not expect that the development of effective systems and processes to support greater participation will always be easy. Indeed it is likely that a number of difficulties will be experienced before a school is able to implement systems of student involvement that are either consistently adhered to or fully effective. Careful preparation for the promotion of student involvement is essential if this is to be anything more than a tokenistic process. Teachers embarking upon a pathway to establish a more student-friendly approach to learning need to be aware of the potential pitfalls. In this chapter we explore some of the challenges of developing student involvement processes in schools and examine some of the ways in which these might be overcome. In particular we consider the skills and conditions required by both adults and students to encourage successful practices and the importance of fostering positive relationships between interested parties.

ATTITUDES AND BELIEFS

In the early chapters of this book we considered the changing nature of teaching and the teacher/student relationship. In so doing, we suggested that there is much to be learned from listening to the voices of students and that this may provide a useful means of supporting effective teaching. In order that student participation in the assessment, planning and evaluation of their own learning can be effectively encouraged and managed, it is necessary to examine both the practical deployment of participatory approaches and those conditions that may either enhance or inhibit them. Of all the factors that influence the development of effective partnerships in learning between adults and students, those embedded in the attitudes and beliefs of teachers are most significant. A commitment to student participation and a belief that such a process is beneficial to learning is an essential prerequisite for the development of increased student involvement. If a teacher lacks this conviction and sees their role simply as that of the expert purveyor of knowledge, rather than a facilitator of learning and a promoter of independence, then the likelihood of creating an environment conducive to student participation is severely impeded.

There are three specific concerns that adults sometimes have with regard to the consideration of student voice (Lundy 2007). These begin with scepticism about the capacity of young people to formulate ideas in a way that enables a meaningful contribution to decision making or evaluation. This perception is particularly prominent in respect of young people who may be labelled as having a special educational need or disability, or who are seen to face other challenges such as those associated with culture or language. A further anxiety experienced by some adults is a concern that the devolution of responsibilities to students may undermine the authority of teachers and result in increased disciplinary problems and an undermining of school stability. Finally, some teachers may find that the establishments of procedures for the promotion of increased student participation and autonomy is time-demanding and likely to prove a distraction from the essential core activities of teaching. Each of these issues comes from a genuine concern of teachers to ensure the maintenance of a professional management of the education of young people and the promotion of a stable school system. Whilst these three concerns may be seen as inhibitors of progress towards the promotion of student participation and increased learner autonomy, it would be unwise to ignore them or to believe that progress can be made without allaying teacher apprehensions. For this reason we will consider each of these concerns in turn and discuss the ways in which teachers and other adults may ensure that student involvement makes a positive contribution to teaching and learning.

Student capacity to contribute

The lack of maturity or limited abilities of students is often cited as an inhibiting factor in the promotion of student involvement in decision making. However, research indicates that children from a very young age are capable of expressing their views based upon an ability to reason about their own experiences and the environment in which they live. Children between the ages of four and seven years engaged in classroom discussion have been shown to be able to think logically and imaginatively, thereby forming opinions and expressing ideas, engaging in well-constructed argument, collaborating and seeing the point of view of others (Drummond 1993). Primary school students from their earliest days of schooling have been found to be able to make judgements about their own performance and to express their ideas and opinions in a cogent manner (Griffiths and Davies 1995). This is not to suggest that students are not relatively naïve at an early age when their experiences are invariably limited. It is clear that the cognitive skills required for abstract reasoning and more sophisticated problem solving or decision making are not present in the youngest children and tend to develop later and with increased experience and learning (Rutter and Rutter 1993). Children appear to move from a 'literal' understanding of the world to an ability to interpret situations and events by generalizing from earlier experiences and developing those patterns and themes which enable them to become increasingly sophisticated and independent of thought (Greenfield 2000). This development of meaning is, of course, important in terms of a student's ability to make evaluations or to predict personal learning needs. It is clearly necessary for teachers to be aware of the differing levels of maturity and needs of students within any classroom. However, it is clear that even prior to entering school most children have developed a level of sophistication as thinkers that enables them to make decisions and express ideas about their own needs.

Expectations surrounding students with special educational needs may have a considerable influence upon their inclusion in decision making and the expression of opinions or ideas. Scepticism about involving such students may manifest itself in the form limiting opportunities for them because of a perception that they are not able to make a valid contribution in determining their own needs or making evaluations of their own performance. These low expectations of students with special educational needs have been challenged by research into the personal target setting abilities of students with severe and complex learning difficulties that has revealed a number of positive factors (Fletcher 2001; Rose 1999). Not least among these was an indication that with careful structuring and the provision of an appropriate learning environment, many such students were able to identify their own learning strengths and weaknesses and make judgements about their progress against pre-set targets. Such involvement is not easily achieved; indeed, the research recommends highly structured approaches to assessing needs and mapping these against curriculum opportunities and classroom management approaches that encourage autonomous learning, as we will discuss later in this chapter. Furthermore, for some students, such as those with profound and multiple learning difficulties or others on the autistic spectrum, there may be additional challenges of identifying appropriate modes of communication to encourage effective participation. However, the dangers of stereotyping are most likely to lead to a lowering of expectations and in some instances may result in teachers not attempting to involve students in the assessment, planning or evaluation of their own learning needs. Part of the challenge of teaching is to discover new approaches that assist learners in overcoming the difficulties they encounter. The more closely students are involved in this process the more likely they are to respond to the demands of the teacher and the more confident they may become as learners.

Effects on teacher authority

Concerns about teacher authority may be closely related to the confidence of individual teachers. The importance of the teacher–child relationship and its role in promoting student participation has been emphasized by several writers (e.g. Beveridge 2004; Griffiths 1996). Certainly teachers need to maintain the respect of the students they teach. However, apprehensions over a lessening of this position when encouraging greater student autonomy would appear to be misplaced. Students who are closely involved in assessment procedures and personal planning related to their learning needs are found to become more accurate in making judgements about their own performance and also become more focused upon classroom activity (Munby 1995).

Psychological empowerment, whereby individuals feel that they have some control over their own circumstances, that they have the skills to achieve desired outcomes and that they can apply those skills to achieve desired outcomes, has been identified as an important contributor to effective learning (Wehmeyer, Agran and Hughes 1998). This may best be achieved when teachers encourage student autonomy and should deliver benefits for the teacher as well as the student. In particular, the student who feels psychologically empowered is more likely to respond positively to the teaching situation and to feel well motivated and confident about learning. This is a state for which many teachers strive but which appears elusive when working with students who may exhibit difficult behaviours or have learning difficulties.

Clearly it demands considerable confidence on the part of the teacher to encourage students to express their views, assess their own learning and play a major role in setting learning targets. Many teachers feel that what they perceive to be the relinquishing of power to students may result in difficult behaviours emanating from student interpretations that they can do as they please. It is important to remember that promoting increased student autonomy does not imply abandoning classroom rules and lowering expectations of conduct (Deci and Chandler 1986). It has been demonstrated how encouraging students to make greater decisions about their own learning needs and then encouraging them to monitor progress can have a positive impact upon student behaviour. For example, when students regulate their own behaviour on the basis of having been involved in its assessment and in setting targets for self-management, they are more likely to respond positively than on occasions when their behaviour is regulated by an adult in a position of authority (Cooper 1993; Kern *et al.* 1994).

Time demands

The concerns of some teachers about the additional time that might be demanded in encouraging student involvement, and the potential distraction from other core classroom activities is an issue that deserves careful consideration. Undoubtedly the setting up of any new initiative in school makes demands upon the time of staff. Teachers lead busy lives, and the pressures of the curriculum and classroom management are such that any changes introduced need to be seen to be beneficial to both students and staff. Research on a national scale conducted in 1996 revealed staff in schools that had implemented systems to promote greater student involvement were able to articulate the advantages that accrue from this action (Rose, McNamara and O'Neil 1996). In particular, they spoke about increased student ownership of assessment and learning, a greater focus upon intended learning outcomes and improved cooperation resulting from the actions taken. However, at that time many teachers regarded student self-assessment and other forms of student involvement as an add-on to the teaching process rather than an integral part of it. In order to ensure that student involvement becomes embedded within classroom procedures teachers require support in developing systems and approaches that are seen to be manageable and beneficial. The approaches described later in this chapter and in chapter 6 have been developed by teachers in schools, who are committed to the principles of student involvement and who have recorded the advantages of implementing participatory approaches.

However, before examining these it is necessary to examine the principles upon which effective student involvement can be based.

ESTABLISHING PRINCIPLES FOR STUDENT INVOLVEMENT

The notion of personalized learning has received support in recent years from a number of government publications. *Removing Barriers to Achievement* (Department for Education and Skills 2004) emphasized the importance of consultation with and involvement of students throughout the learning process by:

- having high expectations of all children
- building on the knowledge, interests and aptitudes of all children
- involving them in their own learning
- developing confidence in children
- helping them to develop skills relevant to their lives.

These five requirements are in alignment with the principles espoused both in international documents such as the United Nations Convention on the Rights of the Child (1989) and in the Special Educational Needs Code of Practice (2001) discussed in chapter 3.

While the idea of personalized learning is encouraging, many teachers may require help in understanding what it might look like in practice (Mortimer 2004). Four overriding principles have been described for communicating with students and involving them in making decisions about their own needs (Mortimer 2004, p.170, summarizing the work of Drummond, Rouse and Pugh 1992):

- Respect each child for their culture, their ethnicity, their language, their religion, their age, their disability and their gender. The methods we choose for communication, assessment and intervention must be appropriate for the child. There must be no danger of bias.
- The care and education of young children are not two separate, discrete activities. In the work done by early years practitioners, quality care is educational and quality education is caring. Therefore, when we communicate with young children, we need to attend to their whole development and lives and not to certain aspects of it.
- Foundation stage practitioners inevitably have 'power' when communicating with children and their families; this needs to be acknowledged and used lovingly, wisely and well.

- Always keep the interests of the child paramount. Assessment and intervention must enhance the child's life, learning and development. It must 'work' for the child and we will *know* that it is working because we are 'listening' to children's voices, with our ears, our eyes and through our ongoing interactions with them.

This focus is upon children in the early years, but these principles hold good for professionals working with children and young people of all ages. They put the student at the centre of learning and are founded upon principles of respect and the development of positive teacher and student relationships. They also identify issues that need further consideration when establishing practices, and that endorse student participation in the classroom. These are useful for any teacher or school endeavouring to create a learning environment conducive to student involvement.

The creation of an ethos of respect is always an important starting point for working with students in school. This requires that teachers not only recognize individuality but also take affirmative actions to celebrate and endorse the personal characteristics of learners. Students are quick to pick up on the sincerity of teachers over their individuality, and this inevitably impacts either positively or negatively upon relationships and can have a considerable impact upon learning. Teachers need to take actions indicating their respect for individual students, which includes:

- making time to listen to the ideas and opinions of students
- taking an interest in those things which most interest students and engaging them in discussion of these
- ensuring that they are informed about the religious or cultural heritage and practices of children
- using language that encourages students to engage in dialogue and that neither patronizes nor makes assumptions of student understanding.

These principles for communication should guide the work of teachers with all students. However, for some it will be necessary to take additional actions and to have an increased awareness of student sensitivities or difficulties. When working with students for whom English is an additional language or with those who have special educational needs, it may be necessary to introduce additional resources supportive of a student's language or an augmentative form of communication. In addressing the needs of such learners, it is essential that teachers maintain high expectations and do not see the challenges of communication as a reason for underachievement or for not consulting and involving the student in assessment and learning processes. This may require that teachers develop new skills and understanding about specific approaches that enable the student to participate fully.

Case study 4.1 Brian: listening, then acting

Brian is a teacher in a primary school working with a class of Year 3 (seven-year-old) students. He has implemented a system in his maths lessons to encourage his students to identify those aspects of the lesson which they have found easy or difficult, and to comment on what helps them to learn. Within his class he has a student who has difficulties with communication and with reading. Brian has ensured that this student can be part of the same lesson evaluation scheme by producing materials focused on his individual needs through use of pictorial representation and symbols.

For the majority of the class Brian uses a simple written evaluation form:

Today in maths we have been working with fractions. We have been dividing shapes into halves and quarters.

Was the lesson   FUN   BORING

Did you find the lesson   EASY   HARD

If you want, write about something which could help you to learn better in maths lessons.

For the student with communication and reading difficulties Brian has produced a modified sheet, which one of the other students reads to him and helps him to complete.

How was maths for you today? (colour one of the faces)

If you want, draw a picture to show how I can help you better in maths lessons.

In his maths lesson Brian has adopted a half-termly summary and action sheet through which he demonstrates to his class that he has listened to their ideas and is prepared to take actions which may help them in learning. An example of Brian's summary and action sheets is presented below.

During this half term you told me that maths was:

Usually fun

Sometimes lessons were too long!

We all need more practice measuring

What shall we do?

We have agreed to have five minutes doing exercises in the middle of maths lessons.

We will practise measuring in science lessons and in art lessons next term.

At the end of each half term Brian summarizes what his pupils have told him and produces this sheet on the interactive whiteboard. He discusses what the pupils have reported through their evaluations with the class and together they decide any changes to make or ideas they want to put in place. In this way Brian demonstrates a commitment to respecting the evaluations made by his class and to taking actions to improve learning opportunities for all his pupils. Through participating in the evaluations and subsequent discussion the class are learning the importance of listening to the views of others and behaving in a democratic manner.

In the example provided above the teacher has not only shown a commitment to student involvement, he has ensured that a student who may have difficulty in participating through conventional means is given appropriate support. Such modification does of course, take time, but is essential when creating a classroom environment conducive to student participation.

It is not suggested that the teacher and student relationship is one of equals. The teacher, whose actions are inevitably influenced by the requirements of the curriculum or a syllabus, has to make decisions and judgements about what is to be taught and how. Teachers have experience and understanding that is different from that of the students they teach and is essential in supporting them in all their learning. The notion of 'power' in the relationship between teachers and pupils (and their families) is an important one and needs to be given due consideration. It is not suggested that teachers should relinquish their authority in the classroom, but rather that they should consider how the decisions they make impact upon the individual learner. In Case study 4.1 the teacher sought to gain the opinions of his class about the effectiveness of his maths lesson. This would have been a fruitless exercise unless he was prepared to take account of the views of his students when planning further maths activity. Simply seeking views without being prepared to reflect upon their meaning and the potential for improving teaching is not a worthwhile exercise. If the teacher is prepared to do this, there is an opportunity to modify teaching in a way that will ensure that students have better access to learning. The teacher will also be showing respect for his or her class and demonstrating that he or she values their ideas and opinions and is prepared to change the approach to meet their needs. If the teacher is not prepared to act in this way, student involvement becomes a tokenistic act, which takes time but has no value as part of a teaching and learning process. Students are quick to recognize such tokenism and are unlikely to respond positively to teachers who lack sincerity in activities of this nature.

As has been said, it is important to keep the interests of the child paramount. We also need to enhance the child's life, learning and development and give full attention to the child's interpretation of their own learning situation (Mortimer 2004). Such a principle should become second nature to teachers as it ensures sensitivity to the needs of the student, which will enable modifications to teaching to be made in order to promote effective learning. However, teachers also need to be aware of the possible tensions and confusions that may prove influential when attempting to increase student participation.

Young children are subjected to a wide range of attitudes and expectations from adults. Some will have encountered situations, either at home or in school, where their opinions have seldom been sought and their ideas largely discarded. Whilst it is impossible for teachers or other adults to achieve consistency in the behaviours of every adult with whom the student comes in to contact, it is essential that consistent behaviour on the part of individual adults is maintained in class and, if possible, across the school. Students from an early age develop an astute sense of justice and a good understanding of the importance of positive and reliable relationships with teachers. This is clearly illustrated by a 12-year-old girl:

> To make a good school I would say you need trust. Trust between a student and a teacher, between students, between teachers, and the whole school. You need fairness; teachers shouldn't show favouritism, they should keep it inside; and students should be expected to behave in lessons and get good treatment back. To be a good teacher you have to be fair by expecting the students to follow your rules and treating them fairly back. (Burke and Grosvenor 2003, p.84)

Such insights are invaluable to the teacher and provide a clear indication of this girl's appreciation of the necessary conditions for learning. The consequences of not building a relationship founded upon mutual trust can be devastating and have a negative impact upon both learning and attitudes towards schooling. The following example of exclusion from effective learning comes from a student who had been diagnosed as dyslexic and clearly felt frustration at being unable to access appropriate support.

> I wouldn't ask for help. You might not be actually told you're stupid, but you're getting the hidden messages, so you're not going to go 'I'm stupid can I have help?' Like, writing down homework from the blackboard was a nightmare for me – I always went home with half

sentences or with the same sentence down three times. (Kenny *et al.* 2000, p.25)

This student clearly lacked any confidence that the teacher would provide a positive response to a request for support. Her low expectations of the teacher may be unfounded, but it is clear that through a lack of opportunity to express her own difficulties and frustrations she is struggling to gain the same learning opportunities as those afforded to her peers. Most schools would suggest that their commitment to equality of opportunity is paramount. This was clearly not seen to be the situation for this young person whose opinions of teachers are likely to be coloured by the experiences described above.

CREATING THE SKILLS FOR PARTICIPATION

Even when teachers are fully committed to the processes of student participation there is no guarantee that this will be easily achieved. Students need to acquire both the confidence and the skills to be able to make decisions and judgements about their own learning. When students first enter school they may lack many of the necessary skills to engage in choice or decision-making processes. These often need to be specifically taught, and teachers need to identify those daily opportunities within normal classroom activities to promote the development of participation skills.

Research has been conducted to examine the skills required by students with severe learning difficulties if they were to be involved in evaluation of their own learning (Rose, Fletcher and Goodwin 1999). The students presented complex learning needs and often expectations were low with regard to their ability to make informed judgements or to evaluate their own progress. Following an analysis of the skills possessed by students who were effective in personal target setting and evaluation of their own learning, the researchers were able to isolate a number of skills that appear to be essential if students are to be effective participants in assessment, planning and evaluation procedures. These skills were identified within three categories – negotiation; self-knowledge and the recognition of personal potential; and prediction skills, including concepts of time, and were seen as essential components of skilled student participation. Observation of students over a prolonged period enabled three checklists of skills to be produced as follows.

Negotiation

- Can state an opinion with confidence
- Can disagree with confidence

- Is able to 'take turns' and wait for own turn
- Takes part in a two-way conversation
- Can say 'Yes' and 'No' in response to requests
- Seeks clarification and help when unable to understand
- Expresses personal feelings and needs
- Maintains and develops a topic of conversation effectively and appropriately
- Stands up for self – can represent own views and feelings in an assertive and non-aggressive way
- Makes suggestions and gives opinions in the correct context
- Has well-developed skills of refusal which are used effectively and appropriately
- Achieves a good balance between listening and responding
- Is able to initiate conversations successfully
- Adapts behaviour and language to the context and listener

Self-knowledge – Recognition of potential

- Recognizes/identifies personal achievements
- Knows when something has been achieved
- Identifies personal strengths and weaknesses
- Identifies likes and dislikes
- Identifies possible future leaving (post-school) needs
- Recognizes having had an effect upon decisions
- Identifies something which cannot be achieved
- Recognizes something which cannot be done yet, but which can be achieved with time
- Identifies possible learning strategies, including the need for support
- Recognizes something which the target setter could not do, but can do now
- Acknowledges and identifies difficulties or non-achievement experienced
- Understands concepts of hard, easy and manageable

Prediction skills – Concept of time

- Understands the concept of time in relation to the target set

- Understands differences in time scales – day/week/term, etc.
- Identifies/recognizes/states the benefits of achieving a target

It was observed that students lacking these skills had difficulties in being effective when engaged in decision-making or target-setting activities. When teachers worked on the development of these skills they found that students became more adept at making judgements, gained in confidence when expressing an opinion and played a more active role in self-evaluation. Students with special educational needs are often regarded as having limited abilities in relation to the skills listed above. However, several special schools for students with severe learning difficulties have adopted these checklists and by assessing student skills and encouraging development where students were perceived to have weaknesses they have succeeded in encouraging greater student autonomy. This has resulted in improvements in student motivation and has encouraged increased self-awareness and confidence in learning. The skills identified appear to be essential for all students, regardless of need or ability; therefore this research is applicable in any situation where teachers are committed to increasing student participation.

It is not suggested that any of the above skills can be taught in a discrete manner. It is, however, possible to identify opportunities within many lessons to promote the development of these skills and to plan for their inclusion within daily classroom routines.

Case study 4.2 Angela: helping a student participate

Angela teaches a class of Year 5 (nine-year-old) students. She is committed to encouraging students to gain a degree of autonomy in learning and wants her class to take increased responsibility for their own learning. All of the students are involved in evaluating their own performance and in setting personal learning targets. Within her class, one student, Andrew, who has Down syndrome, is having some difficulties in participating at the same level as the others in the class. Andrew works hard, is well liked in class but has some difficulties in participating in self-evaluation and planning activities.

Angela has used the checklist of skills to assess how she might be able best to assist Andrew in developing his learning abilities. Andrew has difficulties with several of the skills, and Angela has decided to focus on a couple of these at the end of each day. Towards the end of each afternoon Angela has built a ten-minute evaluation period into her timetable. During this time students come together and discuss, either as a whole class or in groups, how the day has been for them. Each day they focus upon three questions – How well did we work today? What did we learn? and What do we need to do better? During these sessions Andrew has generally had difficulties participating. Angela recognizes that he has difficulties *achieving a good balance between listening and responding* and *knowing when something has been achieved*. In order to begin to overcome these difficulties she has implemented a specific strategy.

During the ten-minute evaluation session Andrew has been allocated a 'buddy'. This is one of his classmates to whom Andrew relates well. The teacher encourages Andrew to listen carefully to his classmates. After a while she makes a point of saying that it is now time to listen to Andrew and his buddy. At this point she asks Andrew about what he has enjoyed today. She then asks his buddy to tell the class one thing that Andrew has done well (achieved) during the day. This may be related to the day's lessons; it could equally be something from the playground or in another social situation. Andrew is then asked to respond to what his buddy has said.

After a few weeks Andrew has learned that this is a regular routine. He has gradually become more confident in responding to the comments of his buddy. He is also listening more carefully to what others are saying and waiting until it is his turn to say something. Each day in class Angela gives Andrew regular reminders to think about what he is learning so that he will have something to say during the evaluation session.

Angela is using daily opportunities to address the skills needed by students to become more effective in evaluating and commenting upon their own learning. She is demonstrating to the whole class that she values their opinions and is also focusing their attention upon their performance both individually and as a whole class. In recognizing that Andrew has some learning difficulties she has decided to improve his personal skills and has shown him that she has high expectations of his participation in activities alongside his peers. This encourages him to work on the skills, that he needs to acquire and also ensures that all members of the class recognize that Andrew is expected to achieve in the same ways as others.

Approaches to pupil involvement such as demonstrated in Case study 4.2 are founded upon a practical approach to ensuring that all learners have access to lessons and are encouraged to participate to their full potential. There have been many instances in the past where pupils have felt excluded from lessons because of an inability to understand the demands of the teachers or to compete with their peers. The approaches presented in this chapter show how with a little thought and preparation it is possible to overcome the exclusion from learning experienced by some pupils.

SUMMARY

In this chapter we have:

- presented a set of principles upon which practical pupil involvement can be developed

- considered the skills, knowledge and understanding that pupils need if they are to be involved fully in decision-making processes

- demonstrated through case studies how schools have developed approaches to involving children in assessment procedures.

REFERENCES

Beveridge, S. (2004) 'Student participation and the home school relationship.' *European Journal of Special Needs Education 19*, 1, 3–16.

Burke, C. and Grosvenor, I. (2003) *The School I'd Like: Children and Young People's Reflections on Education for the 21st Century.* London: Routledge.

Cooper, P. (1993) *Effective Schools for Disaffected Students.* London: Routledge.

Deci, E.L. and Chandler, C.L. (1986) 'The importance of motivation for the future of the learning disabilities field.' *Journal of Learning Disabilities 19*, 4, 587–594.

Department for Education and Skills (2004) *Removing Barriers to Achievement: The Government's Strategy for SEN.* Nottingham: DfES.

Drummond, M.J. (1993) *Assessing Children's Learning.* London: David Fulton.

Drummond, M.J., Rouse, D. and Pugh, G. (1992) *Making Assessment Work: Values and Principles in Assessing Young Children's Learning.* London: National Children's Bureau.

Fletcher, W. (2001) 'Enabling Students with Severe Learning Difficulties to Become Effective Target Setters.' In R. Rose and I. Grosvenor (eds) *Doing Research in Special Education.* London: David Fulton.

Greenfield, S. (2000) *The Private Life of the Brain.* London: Penguin.

Griffiths, M. and Davies, C. (1995) *In Fairness to Children.* London: David Fulton.

Griffiths, T. (1996) 'Teachers and Students Listening to Each Other.' In R. Davie and D. Galloway (eds) *Listening to Children in Education.* London: David Fulton.

Kenny, M., McNeela, E., Shevlin, M. and Daly, T. (2000) *Hidden Voices: Young People with Disabilities Speak about Their Second Level Schooling.* Cork: South West Regional Authority.

Kern, L., Dunlap, G., Childs, K.E. and Clarke, S. (1994) 'Use of a classwide self-monitoring program to improve the behaviour of students with emotional and behavioural disorders.' *Education and Treatment of Children 17*, 3, 445–458.

Lundy, L. (2007) '"Voice" is not enough: conceptualising Article 12 of the United Nations Convention on the Rights of the Child.' *British Educational Research Journal 33*, 6, 927–942.

Mortimer, H. (2004) 'Hearing children's voices in the early years.' *Support for Learning 19*, 4, 169–174.

Munby, S. (1995) 'Assessment and Pastoral Care: Sense, Sensitivity and Standards.' In R. Best, P. Lang, C. Lodge and C. Watkins (eds) *Pastoral Care and Personal Social Education.* London: Cassell.

Rose, R. (1999) 'The involvement of students with severe learning difficulties as decision makers in respect of their own learning needs.' *Westminster Studies in Education 22*, 4, 19–29.

Rose, R., Fletcher, W. and Goodwin, G. (1999) 'Students with severe learning difficulties as personal target setters.' *British Journal of Special Education 26*, 4, 220–226.

Rose, R., McNamara, S. and O'Neil, J. (1996) 'Promoting the greater involvement of students with special needs in the management of their own assessment and learning procedures.' *British Journal of Special Education 23*, 4, 166–171.

Rutter, M. and Rutter, M. (1993) *Developing Minds.* London: Penguin.

Wehmeyer, M.L., Agran, M. and Hughes, C. (1998) *Teaching Self-determination to Students with Disabilities.* Baltimore, MD: Paul H. Brookes.

CHAPTER 5

Student Involvement in Learning through Assessment

In the previous chapter we discussed the need to establish a set of principles that would positively influence student participation. It is clear that progress in this area will not be forthcoming until teachers make a commitment to listening to their students and making use of the information with which they are provided. However, simply having a commitment to greater student involvement is not sufficient to ensure that effective procedures will be put into place or to maximize the benefits of better student participation.

In this chapter, through the use of practical examples, we consider how students may be involved in each stage of the learning process, including planning, assessment and evaluation. In so doing we also discuss how this may be beneficial not just in terms of the academic outcomes for students, but also in respect of the management of student behaviour and social aspects of learning.

THE ROLE OF THE TEACHER

In his seminal work on the development of the curriculum, the American educator Ralph Tyler suggested that education was a process of changing behaviour patterns in people (Tyler 1949). He was, of course, not referring to behaviour in a simplistic sense, but rather concerned for the development of understanding, thinking and emotional responses to the learning environment. This notion of changing people is one that elicits a range of responses. For a start, it implies that teachers work with individuals who need to be changed. Certainly it is the role of teachers to impart knowledge, encourage learners to shape their ideas, to develop confidence and to begin to question their own understanding of the world in which they live. This does not imply a system of indoctrination, but rather guided encouragement of students to explore their own responses, emotions and understanding of an increasingly complex set of ideas and concepts. In the 1961 novel *The Prime of Miss Jean Brodie*, Muriel Spark's feisty teacher declares that:

> The word 'education' comes from the root *e* from *ex* out and *duco*, I lead. It means a leading out. To me education is a leading out of what is already there in the pupil's soul. To Miss Mackay it is a putting in of something that is not there, and that is not what I call education.

The role of the teacher is both complex and subject to the vagaries of legislation, policy and educational trends, which invariably make demands upon the ways in which teachers operate. What is evident is that students like consistency in their teachers in order to understand what is expected of them and to be able to anticipate the responses that will follow their own actions. Teachers need to establish a position of respect and appreciation from their students. This is most readily achieved when the students themselves are clear about the teacher's role and their intentions with regard to teaching and learning. Exploring the role of the teacher and how this is perceived has been a focus of research and debate for many years (e.g. Hanley 2007; Hargreaves 1994; Woods *et al.* 1997). Whilst interpretations of teacher effectiveness vary, a constant factor is the importance of the relationship that teachers establish with their learners. The philosopher Mary Warnock has considered this relationship and how an understanding of the role of the teacher is critical to the development of effective learning.

> Should teachers adopt a godlike role, or even the role of peddler of his wares? Should they not rather allow the pupils to lead in the very definition of the wares themselves? If the ideal of education as a kind of growth (rather than as the receiving of stuff to be consumed) is to be realised, then perhaps we ought to be looking in a rather different direction. For it might be that a condition of growth is self-determination. To be a mere receiver or consumer might be actually stunting. (Warnock 1977, p.57)

Warnock's assertion of the role of the teacher as a facilitator of learning is important and one that we, as authors of this book, would wish to endorse. The quotation above makes clear that an important purpose for the teaching process is the promotion of self-determination in the learner, a move away from dependency to a state of autonomy in respect of learning and decision making. This stance does not detract from the importance of the teacher as a source of knowledge and information. The focus is rather upon the actions of the teacher in encouraging the student to learn and to develop good practices for independent thinking, learning and action. It must surely be a goal of all teachers to enable their learners to become independent in terms of both their ability to study and of decision making based upon their learning and experiences. If this is the case, it is certainly appropriate that teachers should invest time in creating opportunities for their students to take some responsibility for their own learning. Experience of decision making and the acceptance of personal responsibility can only be achieved with practice. In some classes this has been limited through the adoption of teaching practices that are controlling and inhibiting rather than supportive of personal growth and development. This shift of emphasis however, will only be achieved when teachers develop the necessary skills and confidence to concentrate their attentions as much upon pedagogy as on lesson content.

A further factor that has been influential in respect of the approaches of teachers to their learners has been the imposition of labels on students that have a negative impact on their opportunities to access learning; for example, the potentially negative influence of terms such as *special educational needs* or *English as an additional language* on teacher expectations. We are not suggesting that students who experience barriers to learning might not require specialist approaches, additional support or resources or well-differentiated lessons. Rather, we believe that these can be provided within a teaching framework, which encourages student participation and decision making at every stage. In this chapter we consider a vital part of the teaching and learning process, that of assessment and the ways in which teaching may be determined on the basis of principles of assessment that encourage student participation.

Observation

One of the most fundamental aspects of assessment is the observation of students by teachers to improve their understanding of how they learn and of the situations that encourage effectiveness. A systematic approach to observation, allowing for the collation and interpretation of information, can lead to affirmative action to improve teaching and learning. However, observation as a means of obtaining useful information that can be translated into classroom action is often limited because of an insufficient focus on or identification of key questions upon which the observation is based (Tilstone 1998).

A good case can be made for observation, even that of an unstructured nature, but the interpretation of observation data can be problematic and even at times contentious (Clark and Leat 1998). Teacher assessment of students based upon observation of their behaviour or performance is invariably subjective. Two teachers observing the same student in the identical situation may place differing emphases on what they are seeing and may come up with two completely different interpretations of what they have seen. The use of teacher observation will continue to play an important role in our understanding of student behaviour and performance; however, there are times when the involvement of the students themselves in this process may prove valuable.

Case study 5.1 Lisa: involving the student in observation

Lisa is a teacher in a special school for students with social, emotional and behavioural difficulties. She has a class of seven Year 8 and 9 students (ages 13–14 years). Gordon, who joined the group at the beginning of term, is having difficulties settling in the class and making friends. When Lisa has talked to some of the other students in the class they say that Gordon is often rude and aggressive towards them and that they don't like working with him. Gordon has complained to Lisa that the other students in the class don't like him and that they will not be friends.

Lisa asks her teaching assistant Angela to spend half an hour watching her teach an art lesson. The focus of the observation is on Gordon's interaction with his peers. Angela observes the lesson and records Gordon's behaviour and the reactions of his peers to him during the lesson. After the lesson, in discussion with Lisa, Angela reports that on several occasions during the lesson Gordon made negative comments about other students' work. He also refused to share materials with others and became verbally aggressive when they tried to use resources that were intended for use by the whole group. Lisa discussed his behaviour during the lesson with Gordon, but he was unwilling to see anything other than his own point of view.

The following morning Lisa arranges for Angela to video-record a science lesson in which Gordon was a student. During this lesson Gordon's behaviour is similar to that which he had exhibited in the art lesson. Later in the day Lisa makes time to observe the video recording with Gordon. She tells Gordon that she wants him to watch the video and afterwards tell her what he feels about the lesson. She does not specifically mention his behaviour. After watching the video Gordon begins to criticize the other students in the class for not wanting to work with him. Lisa agrees that this is a problem and suggests that they look at part of the video again and try to work out why. This time, during the viewing of the video she asks Gordon questions about his own behaviour in the lesson and the way he interacts with other students. Whilst still wishing to apportion blame on others, Gordon does recognise that sometimes he does things which might annoy other students. In discussion with Gordon they identify one other student in the class, Andrew with whom Gordon would particularly like to form a friendship.

Lisa tells Gordon that she will arrange to video next week's science lesson so that they can look again and see if things have improved. She meets with Andrew and explains that Gordon would really like to be friendly with him and asks him to make a special effort to get to know Gordon better. Prior to the next science lesson she discusses the situation with the science teacher and asks that in the lesson Andrew and Gordon could be located together.

After the lesson Lisa brings Andrew and Gordon together to view the video. She focuses attention upon the things that they did well together, and encourages them to discuss how things went and what they liked about the lesson. Whilst Andrew still has some apprehensions about working with Gordon, he recognizes that the lesson was an improvement on the previous week and that Gordon did not stop him from working.

Lisa asks Andrew to tell the whole class about the science lesson and what he liked about working with Gordon. Gordon tells the class about Andrew and how he had helped him with his work. The whole class recognizes that Gordon had been less disruptive and more cooperative in the lesson. Lisa tells the class that she is pleased with the way they have reacted and lets them know that she will be monitoring this situation over the coming weeks.

In Case study 5.1, Lisa could have conducted her own observations and come to conclusions about Gordon's behaviour. Her professional skills and experience as a teacher would have enabled her to reach legitimate conclusions about the classroom situation. By involving Gordon in this process she has not only conducted her own assessment of the situation but has given him some ownership and responsibility for interpreting events in the classroom. Through her actions Lisa has achieved a number of important objectives. First, she has developed a clearer picture of a troublesome situation in her classroom – an essential stage towards tackling a problem. Second, she has communicated to Gordon her concerns about this situation but has done so in a manner that encourages a dialogue and may ultimately enable him to take some responsibility for his own behaviour and learning. Finally, she has engaged other members of her class in a discussion of the situation and through her negotiations with Andrew has put into place a process of attempting to improve matters for the good of all.

This case study does not suggest that there is a quick fix for difficulties such as those experienced by Lisa in her classroom. Addressing social difficulties and those associated with behaviour is always going to be challenging. However, Lisa has adopted a set of principles which, through respecting her students, places her in a position of expecting a degree of cooperation in return. Commanding the respect of students and expecting them to take responsibility for their own actions is more likely to be achieved when they are fully engaged in processes of assessment. This approach may be equally well adopted by teachers working with students in the early years of education, with dialogue between adults and young people that is both respectful and equitable being a key learning tool for all concerned (Murray 2005). In working in this way teachers are required to consider their own behaviours and actions as well as those of the student. This reflective approach enables teachers to gain greater insights into the lives of the young people in their charge (see also Palaiologou 2008).

The process of observation enables teachers to get nearer to an understanding of children and the dynamics of the classrooms in which they work. Observation of an individual pupil, when carefully structured and with a clear purpose, can assist the teacher in gaining an understanding of when actions take place, who they involve and why they may occur. Moreover, carefully planned observations can provide an effective way of gaining insights from pupils themselves about those factors which impact most upon learning (Luff 2007).

PUPIL SELF-ASSESSMENT

Whilst Case study 5.1 considered how one teacher had involved a pupil in observation in order to address social development and the pupil's behaviour, there are, of course, many other ways in which teachers can gain insights into the needs of their class. Pupil self-assessment of learning can assist teachers not only in attaining insights into pupils' learning, but also in planning to move them forward. In order that the process of pupil self-assessment is effective, teachers need to create the right climate of confidence in which pupils will feel that their own opinions can have an impact upon what happens in the classroom. They need to feel confident that if in assessing their own work they identify that they are having difficulties, this will not be interpreted by the teacher as a sign of failure but rather as an effective way of taking some responsibility for personal learning and an important means of seeking help.

In Case study 5.2 we see a teacher who is committed to personal professional development through a process of reflection upon his own classroom performance. In recognizing that some of the pupils in his class are having difficulties, this teacher, rather than assuming that the problems are within the children who are struggling in maths lessons, shows a commitment to changing his own practices in order to help all learners. This inclusive approach is developed by recognizing that all pupils, and indeed all teachers, need extra help from time to time and that it is appropriate to seek assistance. The teacher is focused upon ensuring that pupils feel comfortable in lessons and have the confidence to admit when they are having difficulties and to know that he will respond in a way that is supportive.

Case study 5.2 Simon: implementing a self-assessment system

Simon teaches a Year 4 class (nine-year-olds) in a primary school. The students in his class have a range of needs and abilities. In maths lessons he has become concerned that some of the pupils appear to be finding the acquisition of new mathematical concepts difficult. Whilst he is confident that he is able to identify those students who are having the greatest difficulties, he has become aware that others who he thought were doing well are possibly also struggling. Simon does his best to get around the whole class checking understanding and looking at students' work during maths lessons. However, he is not confident that he is always successful in identifying those students in need of extra help.

In discussion with his class Simon introduces a system of traffic lights which enable his students to make self-assessments of their understanding and performance during maths lessons. He gives each student three discs, coloured red, amber and green. When working independently or in groups during a maths lesson, pupils are encouraged to display one of these discs in front of them. If they display a green disc it means that they are managing the work without difficulty and understand what they are doing. When students display an amber disc it means that they are doing okay but would like some help or to have their understanding checked. When a red disc is displayed it indicates that a student is struggling and unable to manage the work.

Simon is very conscious of the fact that some students may be reluctant to admit that they are struggling, whilst others may simply use the discs to seek attention. He overcomes this difficulty in two ways. First, he discusses the use of the discs regularly with his class. He explains that everybody needs help sometimes, including himself, and that there is nothing wrong with asking for help. Second, he makes a note of all those students who constantly display green discs and checks their work to see if they are consistently performing well. In the odd case where student work does not correlate to their assertion that they need no help, he spends time with these students discussing their work and also their use of the discs.

Simon has found that after a few weeks the students use the discs very sensibly. He is now much more confident that he is able to target those students who need most help during maths lessons in the classroom.

The simple system put into place by the teacher in Case study 5.2 encourages students to involve themselves in decision making about their own performance. Furthermore, it enables them to see that there is a mechanism whereby they can obtain more help when they most need it. The teacher became more confident about his own teaching through the implementation of a process that has made minimal demands upon his own planning but has yielded a positive result. Having identified a personal concern over his recognition of which pupils needed additional assistance in maths lessons, he provided pupils with the confidence to ask for help when needed. The system is relatively simple but gave a clear message to pupils that their own opinions matter and can influence the ways in which the teacher would respond to their needs.

In some schools the principles of pupil self-assessment have been taken forward for pupils with special educational needs into the annual review process. The statutory requirements for pupil progress in relation to the objectives specified in a statement of special educational needs to be reviewed at least annually are enshrined within the Special Needs Code of Practice (Department for Education and Skills 2001). This requires that wherever possible pupils should be actively involved in the review process and should attend all or part of the meeting. It is suggested that they should be actively encouraged to present their own views on their progress over the course of the year. This level of involvement can be daunting both for the pupil, and for adults involved in annual review procedures. Whilst we would certainly advocate that pupils should be fully involved in their annual reviews, we would urge teachers to be conscious of the potential challenges this presents and to spend an appropriate amount of time in preparing all parties for this procedure.

When considering how pupils may be involved in annual reviews, there is a need for careful preparation of the individual pupil concerned. The pupil should be clear about the purpose of the meeting, who will be there, what is likely to happen and what contribution the individual pupil can make. The advantages of involvement are clear, but it is not a simple process and requires a considered approach (Hayes 2004). Adults are generally positive about the involvement of young people in the review process, but we would suggest that it is important to give some particular attention to the feelings of parents in this situation. In some instances parents may feel uncomfortable if the views expressed by their child do not accord with their own. This is not to suggest that this is a reason not to include the pupil in the annual review, but rather to indicate the need for preparation not only of the pupil, but also the parents in some circumstances.

Case study 5.3 Susie: preparing for the annual review

Susie is a Year 6 pupil (ten years old) who attends a junior school. She enjoys school, is sociable and has lots of friends. However, Susie, who has Down syndrome, has some difficulties with learning and has a statement of special educational needs. At the end of this academic year Susie will transfer to a local secondary comprehensive school, and whilst she is looking forward to this her parents have some apprehensions that this transition may prove problematic. Susie is used to being in a small school and having one teacher for most lessons. Next year she will be in a school with 1200 pupils and will have different teachers for each subject.

Susie's teacher Rashida has been preparing her for her forthcoming annual review meeting. She is aware that this meeting will be attended by the head of Year 7 from the secondary school as well as Susie's parents and several other professionals who are involved with her. Rashida wants to involve Susie fully in the annual review and is keen that the meeting concentrates on what Susie has achieved throughout her time at primary school and particularly during the past school year.

Well in advance of the meeting Rashida compiles a list of who will be present. She spends time with Susie talking about each of the individuals concerned and their role in Susie's life. Most of those who will be in attendance are already known to Susie; however, she is unfamiliar with the head of year from the secondary school. Rashida contacts the secondary school and obtains a few details of the year head and also a photograph of him. This enables Rashida to contextualize the situation and to help Susie to gain some confidence about who will be there.

Whilst Susie is quite articulate she tends to be nervous when talking to an audience of adults with whom she is unfamiliar. Rashida therefore decides to assist Susie by helping her to make a PowerPoint presentation to be used during the review. This comprises a series of bullet points and pictures illustrating Susie's achievements during her past year at school. Some show academic achievements, illustrated for example by an extract of a report which Susie wrote following a school visit to the local museum. Others show more personal achievements, including a picture of her receiving a certificate at the local St John Ambulance Brigade where she is a member, and one of her participating in a school netball tournament. She also has slides illustrating the targets set at her last annual review and how these have been addressed. Once the presentation is put together Susie is encouraged to present this to her classmates who ask her questions and give her some feedback on what they have seen.

Rashida encourages Susie to add two particular slides at the end of her presentation. The first of these provides a self-assessment of those aspects of schooling in which she feels confident and others where she feels she needs more help. The second slide lists Susie's aspirations in respect of her move to the secondary school. These are presented here.

At school I am good at these things
Art, music, drama, cooking, working with other people, listening to other people

I am not so good at
Maths and science

I like to have
Pictures as well as words, a buddy to work with, teachers
who listen

When I go to my new school

I would like
To be in the same class as Rachel and Amy
To have a teacher who I can talk to if I have problems
To visit the school with my teacher Mrs Kaur before I come in September

---

A copy of the PowerPoint presentation is sent out with other papers prior to the meeting. This enables all of the adults in attendance to read Susie's work and to be able to discuss this with her at the meeting. All of the adults who will attend are asked to forward any questions they may have for Susie in advance of the meeting. This allows Rashida to discuss these questions and to help Susie to prepare for the discussion that will take place. At the annual review meeting Rashida introduces Susie before she makes her presentation. She has also prepared Susie with a list of questions related to her aspirations, which she is able to ask everyone present in the meeting.

In Case study 5.3 we can see how the pupil is supported in expressing her own views and making a valuable contribution to her annual review meeting. The teacher recognizes the importance of presenting achievements rather than simply focusing upon special educational needs. She is also acknowledging that the pupil has insights into her own learning that can provide valuable information to the other adults present and can contribute to a successful transition from primary to secondary school. The teacher knows that her pupil would lack the confidence simply to attend her annual review and talk about her achievements and aspirations without the support of the visual presentation materials. She also recognizes that by sending the materials to the adults involved in the annual review she is drawing attention to the importance of the girl's own opinions and ideas and assisting them to gain a better picture of what she has achieved. The majority of adults are aware of the need to be supportive of pupils with special educational needs in situations such as these and being well prepared in advance makes life easier for them as well as for the pupils involved.

PEER ASSESSMENT

In addition to encouraging pupils to assess their own learning, teachers often find advantages in encouraging peer assessment. In peer assessment pupils are encouraged to comment upon the work of their classmates and to make observations on how they are performing. In order for this to be successful teachers need to set guidelines for pupils on the purposes of peer assessment and on the need to be fair and to have regard for the feelings of others during the process. The skilled teacher will be aware of which pupils are most likely to find this difficult and may need to manipulate situations in order to ensure the creation of a supportive environment. However, most children have a well-developed sense of fairness and justice and are likely to provide an honest opinion whilst taking account of the sensitivities of others.

Peer assessment can be described in terms of three specific actions (Kelly 2007), these being where the assessor:

- talks about the other child's work in relation to specific success criteria
- makes the other child feel good by pointing out what they have done well

- suggests to the other child how he or she could improve the work.

These three actions should provide an important focus of peer assessment for teachers who are going to introduce this approach. In most instances teachers will pair pupils for assessment activities of this kind and will encourage individuals to make comments to their partner and to the teacher. This process encourages important skills in pupils, such as taking turns, listening carefully to another individual and appreciating sensitivities (Kelly 2007). All of these are skills we would hope to engender in learners, but they are sometimes difficult to achieve.

Peer assessment does not always need to be managed on a one-to-one basis as Case study 5.4 demonstrates.

Case study 5.4 Pauline: peer assessment in groups

Pauline teaches a class of Year 2 and 3 children in a village primary school. For many activities in her class children work in groups. On Tuesday mornings she teaches literacy to her class and sets them groupwork to complete in mixed ability groups. At the end of the morning she gathers the whole class together and encourages them to report on how the group has worked and what they have achieved.

For example, today in the lesson each group has been asked to work together to write and illustrate a poem about the pet they would like. This follows a discussion about why people keep pets and about the animals that various members of the class have at home. Pauline read several poems about animals to the class before setting them the group task. For today's groupwork session she has asked one Year 3 pupil from each group to record what everyone in that group does and to pay particular attention to what they think was done well or what could be improved. She gives the pupils a sheet to record their views on and tells them that they will use these at the end of the morning. The following is a copy of the sheet as completed by a pupil from one of the groups.

What did the group do?

We wrote a poem about dogs and why they are our favourite pets

What did children in the group learn?

We had to learn some spellings and use the dictionary

We had to find rhyming words

We learned about why dogs are good pets

What was the group good at doing?

Drawing the pictures

Thinking of rhyming words

What did the group find difficult?

Getting started

Finding some rhyming words

At the end of the morning the teacher brings all the class together and asks the Year 3 child who was assessing each group to report on what they had recorded. The teacher discusses with them why they found certain aspects of the lesson more difficult than others and how they addressed these difficulties. She encourages each group to assess how well they worked and how effective they were at overcoming difficulties. She then asks each group to go back to their table and write down one thing which they will do in future literacy lessons which might help every one to work better. The group illustrated in the Year 3 pupil's assessment above wrote: *Next lesson if we take turns at saying what we should do, we will find it easier to start writing.*

The teacher takes each group's ideas and writes them on cards which she then gives them at the start of their next literacy group work activity. At the end of that lesson she asks them whether they have worked better and talks to them about what they have achieved.

In Case study 5.4 we see a teacher who is teaching her pupils about the importance of team work. She is encouraging her pupils to respect the opinions of others in the group and enabling them to take some responsibility for their own learning. The teacher maintains careful control of the situation by setting the assessment agenda and providing pupils with the means to conduct the work. However, she is also showing them that she respects their ideas and is prepared to let them take some decisions about their own learning priorities.

In each of the case studies presented in this chapter we have attempted to emphasize that pupil involvement in self-assessment is not about teachers abrogating responsibilities or letting pupils take over the learning agenda, but is rather focused upon encouraging pupils to take some responsibility for their own learning. The advantages that accrued to individuals or groups of pupils in the examples given are clearly related to either behaviour or learning, which are, of course, intrinsically related. Where pupils feel respected and listened to they are more likely to want to work well in order to please the teacher or to meet targets they themselves have identified as important. When such a focus is achieved, it is likely that positive behaviour will follow.

SUMMARY

In this chapter we have:

- considered how pupils can be involved in self-assessment in various ways
- examined how some of the principles of pupil involvement discussed in earlier chapters can be put into practice
- considered how self-assessment may impact upon pupil behaviour
- further discussed the need to enable pupils to take more responsibility for their own learning within an environment of trust and respect created by the teacher.

REFERENCES

Clark, C, and Leat, S. (1998) 'The Use of Unstructured Observation in Teacher Assessment.'
    In C. Tilstone (ed.) *Observing Teaching and Learning.* London: David Fulton.

Department for Education and Skills (2001) *Special Educational Needs Code of Practice.* London: HMSO.

Hanley, U. (2007) 'Fantasies of teaching: handling the paradoxes inherent in models of practice.' *British Educational Research Journal 33,* 2, 253–271.

Hargreaves, A. (1994) *Changing Teachers, Changing Times.* London: Cassell.

Hayes, J. (2004) 'Visual annual reviews: how to include pupils with learning difficulties in their educational reviews.' *Support for Learning 19,* 4, 175–180.

Kelly, P. (2007) 'The joy of involving pupils in their own assessment.' In D. Hayes (ed.) *Joyful Teaching and Learning in the Primary School.* Exeter: Learning Matters.

Luff, P. (2007) 'Written observations or walks in the park: documenting children's experiences.'
    In J. Moyles (ed.) *Early Years Foundations: Meeting the Challenge.* Buckingham: Open University Press.

Murray, J. (2005) 'Studying Children.' In T. Waller (ed.) *An Introduction to Early Childhood.* London: Paul Chapman.

Palaiologou, I. (2008) *Childhood Observation.* Exeter: Learning Matters.

Spark, M. (1961) *The Prime of Miss Jean Brodie.* London: Macmillan.

Tilstone, C. (1998) *Observing Teaching and Learning.* London: David Fulton.

Tyler, R.W. (1949) *Basic Principles of Curriculum and Instruction.* Chicago, IL: University of Chicago Press.

Warnock, M. (1977) *Schools of Thought.* London: Faber and Faber.

Woods, P., Jeffrey, B., Trotman, G. and Boyle, M. (1997) *Restructuring Schools, Restructuring Teachers.* Buckingham: Open University Press.

CHAPTER 6

Planning for Progress and Transition

Periods of transition, between schools or from school to post-school life, often present major challenges to students. This chapter will focus upon how through the involvement of students in planning it is possible to build confidence and enable them to feel in greater control of their lives. The chapter will consider critical events in student lives, such as individual education planning, and suggest how schools may develop principles to support both teachers and students in making the most of opportunities for greater inclusion in school and the wider society in which they will live.

Ensuring that children and young people are active participants in planning for their learning needs is a critical component of an ongoing process that can enable young people to have a degree of control over the direction of their future lives. To an increasing extent policy and practice in relation to children's participation in decision-making processes that affect their lives has evolved considerably:

> We want children and young people...to be able to make a difference. (Children and Young People's Unit 2001, p.1)

> Children and young people with special educational needs have a unique knowledge of their own needs and circumstances and their own views about what sort of help they would like to help them make the most of their education. They should, where possible, participate in all the decision-making processes that occur in education including the setting of learning targets and contributing to IEPs, discussions about choice of schools, contributing to their assessment of needs

and to the annual review and transition process. (Department for Education and Skills 2001, p.27)

However, for all children and young people, and especially those who may be labelled as having special educational needs, the presumption of competence required for active participation in these processes is often questioned and in some cases denied altogether. Some children, as a direct result of their particular learning need, 'may be seen as undeserving of the right to self-advocacy; others, even at secondary level may be perceived as incapable of contributing rationally to decisions about their own lives' (Wearmouth 2001, p.47).

Facilitating pupil participation in decision-making processes is complex and, while professionals generally accept the principle, implementing it can prove difficult. Children from within a social services context have reported that in practice they have a token role within these processes; all the important decisions are taken by the adults and these children felt frustrated and disempowered (Children in Scotland 2006). Their perception of how involved they were in the decision-making process was not solely determined by a successful outcome. Rather their views were influenced by whether they had a reasonable understanding of the procedures involved and whether adults treated their views with respect. Participants, both children and adults, shared similar concerns about the inadequacies of decision-making processes:

> inadequate preparation; a tension between a child-centred agenda and a professional-centred one; language or procedures that children find confusing, boring or off-putting; and, the lack of effective tools, skills and methods for use with young and/or less verbally-adept children. (Children in Scotland 2006, p.6)

Adults involved in facilitating meaningful participation in critical decision-making processes that have major consequences for the lives of these young people need to observe the following principles (Thomas 2002):

- competence presumed
- children's understandings diverge with their experiences
- ability to participate in decision making enhanced with practice
- allowing child to exercise some control over process can have psychological benefits for development
- worry and anxiety can have big impact on ability to participate.

Consultation with children can move from listening to their views towards a model where children are actively involved in the decision-making process and adult power is shared with children (Shier 2001). Setting up this type of process will involve adults asking the following key questions:

> What kind/level of participation am I trying to achieve?
>
> Am I prepared to do this?
>
> What do I need to do in order to make it happen?
>
> How does it become embedded in the work of the organisation?
>
> (Children in Scotland 2006, p.10)

Pupils need support to express their views cogently, and there is ample evidence that with teacher understanding these pupils can become active participants in crucial decisions that will have an impact on the rest of their lives. Practitioners can do the following to ensure participation (MacConville 2007):

- actively look for pupil competence
- not assume their incompetence
- use ways of communication that pupils find helpful
- give pupils time to express views in own way.

Preconceptions about capacity have to be set aside and, in particular for disabled children or others who may have been subjected to traumatizing experiences, teachers need to recognize that these children are 'by no means passive in the construction of their own identities within the social context. These are not the passive, vulnerable children of the Dickensian novel or the socio-medical research literature' (Priestley 1999, p.98).

Actively seeking the views of children and young people with disabilities and/or special educational needs was regarded as a very positive development by the following speaker who has a disability:

> Yeah, people will learn – it's good. People don't ask their opinions because they think they're thick, they're not though. It's a brilliant idea; it'll make life a lot better if they did, to facilitate them and all that. (O'Donnell 2003, p.247)

INDIVIDUAL EDUCATION PLANNING

Individual education planning for children and young people has become an established feature of school provision for the past 30 years. Despite the longevity of this approach to meeting individual needs, many questions remain about the effectiveness and appropriateness of this response, in particular, in relation to the active participation of the young people of concern in this process. Given the increasingly bureaucratic mechanism involved in devising Individual Education Plans (IEPs), it is hardly surprising that the pupil perspective can be compromised by the procedural concerns and the complexity of the process as 'the process of assessment and diagnosis construes the student in a passive way in the sense that experts classify their learning needs' (Hamilton 2009, p.233).

In the United Kingdom IEPs are required under the framework of the Special Educational Needs Code of Practice (Department for Education and Skills 1994, revised in 2001). Increasingly, a similar approach is being adopted with other children who may have social needs. Similar requirements are contained in Republic of Ireland legislation (Education for Persons with Special Educational Needs Act 2004) and policy guidance (Department of Education and Science 2007):

> Students with SEN should be involved in the development, implementation and review of their education plans and learning programmes, where appropriate. They should be given an opportunity to contribute to the setting of targets and to assessment of their progress. (Department of Education and Science 2007)

Pupil contribution to the IEP process is characterized by dialogue and collaboration and the consequent emphasis on the child's strengths and abilities 'provides insight into what the child can do in designated skill areas and what skills the teacher can capitalise on and incorporate into teaching strategies' (National Council for Special Education 2006, p.32). It was never intended that IEPs should be 'just bits of paper, recording measurable and sometimes meaningless targets in the absence of ownership or involvement of the person potentially most willing and able to put in the energy needed to achieve them -the child him or herself' (Gross 2000, p.128). The original intention behind IEPs consisted of bringing together all the people centrally involved in the child's education and enabling children to begin to take charge of their own learning (Gross 2000).

Acknowledging pupil strengths provides an ideal starting point for subsequent involvement in learning plans. Exemplars that emphasize pupil strengths are presented in the *Guidelines on the Individual Education Plan Process* (National Council for Special Education 2006), as outlined below for Luke who is 13 years old and has Asperger syndrome:

General Description

He (Luke) is a second-year student in the local community school, where his older brother is in sixth year. He attends school regularly even though he finds the social aspect and much of the academic work challenging. His favourite subjects are Metalwork and Art. Luke's parents keep in regular contact with the school. At weekends Luke goes fishing with his grandfather. He has won several prizes in local competitions.

Strengths

- Very honest and reliable
- Takes responsibility at home and in school when tasks clearly explained
- Excellent attendance and timekeeping
- Able to work with partner when selection made by teacher
- Keeps to safety rules in labs and workshops
- Well developed visual and spatial skills
- Talented in Art, Metalwork and Technical Graphics
- Excellent memory for factual information
- Dedicated to special interest – fishing

IEP provision in the UK has become firmly embedded within school procedures and, while there have been difficulties with excessive paperwork demands, effective IEP provision can make a significant contribution towards the development of inclusive learning environments. Appropriate IEP processes can embody inclusive principles (Tod 1999):

- a focus on pupil outcomes
- Special Educational Needs embedded in school practice
- pupil and parent involvement.

Developing inclusive learning environments requires a shift from the traditional emphasis on environmental and curricular access towards creating opportunities for pupil engagement in all aspects of school life (Tod 1999).

Within an inclusive learning environment the IEP process becomes a natural outcome of pupil consultation. From the outset, children and young people with disabilities and/or special educational needs are intimately involved; they help to plan the IEP meeting; they decide on the nature of their involvement in the process; they receive support, where necessary, to express their views, their contribution is acknowledged and they are recognized as capable of discussing their choices (Woolfson *et al.* 2006).

In Case study 6.1 individual planning is modelled by the teacher as an ongoing process to enhance communication and empower a young boy within his learning environment.

Case study 6.1 Steven: re-conceptualizing the learning environment

Steven had been diagnosed at three with a dual diagnosis of hearing impairment and autism, and Steven and his family encountered difficulties in accessing appropriate education. Early intervention was mired in conflict as to which intervention Steven should receive. Should he receive interventions in sign language or speech, developmental or behavioural approaches? Steven attended the deaf school with a trained sign language teacher. However, Steven's behaviour became very difficult, isolating him from the other deaf children, and eventually he was enrolled in a mainstream school. While Steven had difficulties communicating and relating he also experienced sensory-processing difficulties. A teacher was employed within the mainstream school to develop appropriate educational provision for Steven when he was six years old.

Steven lived in a silent world, his calm composure showing little response to voice, gesture or sign. In isolation, neither the hearing strategies nor the autism interventions were sensitive to Steven's needs; what was needed was responsive collaboration and access to resources for both. Steven floated on the edge of different worlds challenged by sensory stimuli; unable to connect motor and sensory experiences; failing to develop and integrate schema. Steven's difficulties with sensory processing often led to misperceptions, related to under-, or over-stimulation and, occasionally, anxiety. These difficulties accounted for an inability either to self-regulate or to interact with the world. Steven's organizational difficulties required predictable events and interactions – knowing what was going to happen, and when. The ability to process noise, chaos, a change in events or activities required a high degree of structure and planning. Continuous monitoring of Steven's levels of alertness and motor praxis acted as a guide for the introduction of new concepts.

Using developmental constructs, I checked if Steven responded to the world around him with interest and pleasure. It was necessary to develop a secure attachment in order for him to learn to regulate his emotions and behaviours. Reciprocal exchange of gestures, smiles and emotions encouraged shared interactions. Intensive interaction involves focusing on the child's existing repertoire of communication strategies including sounds, gestures and body language.

Following the principles of Intensive Interaction my imitation of Steven's body language, sounds and movements became efforts to communicate with him. Based on how mothers and babies communicate, Intensive Interaction uses a model of typical development to guide education and socialization, valuing and respecting the child's communicative attempts and using them as our first conversations. It also allowed Steven to take control, while I tuned into the rhythm of his gestures and actions, monitoring my responses. Absence of task allowed me to teach the conversational (verbal and non-verbal) rules of joint attention, turn-taking and intentional behaviour. Steven was given the skills to initiate, reciprocate and sustain interactions.

Cognitively, I felt elements of Steven's capacity were at the sensori-motor stage. I needed to present early learning in experiential format, without the added stress of language. In terms of affect, I modelled and encouraged positive displays of expression, in efforts to increase engagement and enhance resilience. Sessions were highly interactive and designed to stimulate multi-sensory learning.

Our next stage of intervention focused on the functional aspects of communication. Our activities focused on Steven developing a sense of self, relating his needs through language and the encouragement of representational play. It was important that Steven began to integrate planning, problem solving and emotional regulation as well as increasing competencies across multiple domains. It was important to monitor my emotional tone and reactivity, when teaching Steven to wait and attend. When Steven showed signs of functional use of language, we focused on developing a more organized structure to his learning.

So, how did we communicate with Steven? It was essential that we didn't discriminate because of absence of usual forms of communication – absence of words is not an inability to communicate. It was also important that we didn't form misconceptions based on Steven's communication idiosyncrasies and behaviour difficulties. Behaviour was reframed as the communication of needs, wants, pain and attention. Primarily I based our early communication on Steven's non-verbal communication – his sounds, eye-contact, facial expressions, gestures and pointing, and his ability to lead me to something he wanted or needed. During work on curricular concepts, we worked within a hierarchy of concrete concepts moving from representational to abstract, reinforcing the need for all to reach mastery and incorporating the use of augmentative communication techniques. Augmentative communication involves the use of high/low technology to enable people with communication difficulties to communicate more effectively. Assigning meaning, intent and purpose to any of Steven's efforts at communication was essential. Our relationship became more communication partners and less teacher and student. Early efforts at communication centred around items that Steven wanted or liked. Commonly requested picture categories were food and drink, play activities, including favourite toys, books and videos. Pictures of 'yes', 'no' and 'choice' were also introduced.

APPROACHING LEARNING

We approached literacy as a social encounter. Steven began to interpret and use a sign and symbol system. It was important to shift the emphasis from hearing impaired to visually skilled – from deficit to strength. Steven related to the world through his eyes. He needed to access a linguistic environment through different means. Steven initially appeared not to have access to phonological codes, and for this reason we had to explore the concept of literacy outside of the conventional parameters, replacing the ear with the eye. We also had to be mindful that the acquisition of phonological skills through exposure to language, even when the auditory experience is poor, cannot be underestimated. Our capacity to engage with Steven in the visual world was a challenge for us as educators. The goal was to help Steven map between sign and print, and with the help of an interpreter we presented text, finger spelling, graphics and exposure to writing in efforts to create a language-rich environment. It was essential to step back and evaluate the core competencies of a visually literate person. Ensuring an image-rich environment enforced in part by digitally created images addressed Steven's preferred learning style.

A consistent theme was to differentiate instruction by teaching to different modalities, highlighting the prominence of visual literacy, but also incorporating a multi-sensory approach throughout flexible instruction. While most teaching is done through visual and auditory senses, helping Steven to learn through more than one of his senses was challenging but successful. In Steven's case, image, sign and action were not just supports to language as the dominant mode of learning – they were learning itself. Setting learning goals that required visual or sign responses was the key to success for Steven. Kinaesthetic and tactile experiences also allowed Steven to encounter elements of literacy and numeracy. Drawing, use of body and balance, graphics and immersion in air, sand, play-dough, paint and clay were designed to provide a stimulating multi-sensory experience. In efforts to connect early numeracy to real-world events, develop a number sense and encourage automaticity, Steven's learning was facilitated by a combination of direct instruction, situated learning, task-based approaches and a social process co-constructing knowledge.

VOICE

While all voices were valuable in understanding the issues surrounding the integration of a deaf student into a mainstream school, essentially it was a complex undertaking to locate Steven's voice, and more specifically to locate where Steven's voice merged with that of teachers and interpreters. Strategies to develop empowerment, responsibility, choice, reflection and affirmation provided opportunities to find his voice. Re-conceptualizing the learning environment means that educators can provide opportunities for students to become contributors, problem solvers and partners. A major aim of our focus was to provide Steven with the skills needed for effective communication and peer interaction. Allowing Steven to act as agent invited the co-construction of meaning with the intention of developing a dialogue. This re-conceptualization requires a deeper understanding; engagement in a process; learning to listen to a different voice.

TRANSITION

Schools have a mandatory duty to address transition issues, and this area is considered through the Ofsted inspection process. Transition processes for all children can be smooth or problematic, depending on the nature of the transition and the prior preparation and planning. For many children the transition from primary to secondary schooling represents a major challenge and can be a source of anxiety. Children are often concerned about peer relations, in particular making friends and the possibility of bullying, as well as adapting to the increased complexity of routines within secondary schools (McCauley 2009). Successful transition involves five key aspects (Evangelou *et al.* 2008):

- developing new friendships and improving self-esteem and confidence
- settling well in school life such as to cause no concerns to parents
- showing an increasing interest in school and school work
- getting used to new routines and school organization with great ease

- experiencing curriculum continuity.

While children with special educational needs have been shown to be as likely to settle in to secondary school as their peers without special educational needs, they can experience particular difficulties associated with their health, social adjustment and learning needs:

> More specifically, children with special educational needs were more likely to have problems with bullying and there were more worries about them being able to adjust to having different teachers; both factors significantly and directly linked with a successful transition. (Evangelou *et al.* 2008, p.26).

Children with special educational needs can be subjected to more peer rejection (Tur-Kaspa 2002) and are judged by their teachers to be more socially unskilled and exhibiting more problem behaviour than their non-special educational needs classmates. Poor transitions can have negative consequences for educational attainment and pupil well-being (West, Sweeting and Young 2008). Pupils of lower ability and those with low self-esteem appear to experience more stress about transition and often feel ill-prepared (Chedzoy and Burden 2005). Pupils with special educational needs are more likely to be bullied than their peer group (Evangelou *et al.* 2008) There is general agreement that at-risk pupils require a planned intervention prior to transition. Secondary schools may initially characterize the transition process as pastoral care while the ultimate aim is to: 'create secure and settled individual children who would then be able to engage in academic work to the fullest possible extent' (Evangelou *et al.* 2008, p.41).

Particular individuals with special educational needs may experience enhanced difficulties in making a successful transition. For example, young people with attention deficit hyperactivity disorder may find themselves less able to function autonomously within a more complex environment with more exacting demands and routines. These young people are 'likely to need practically oriented support from adults, together with opportunities for the young person to achieve and have their success validated by adults' (Thompson, Morgan and Urquhart 2003, p.93).

In Case study 6.2 Christy, a 14-year-old boy with Asperger syndrome, is enabled to make his transition to a secondary school through a combination of his mother's advocacy and the recognition of his learning and social needs by key personnel in both primary and secondary schools. Christy's voice is evident in the articulation of his needs.

Case study 6.2 Christy: reducing transition anxieties

Prior to the transition Christy's mother was invited to take part in a structured interview about the transition process. Her main worries were related to the specific difficulties experienced by her son, how these might impact on the transition and the likelihood that he would remain in mainstream education. She identified his main difficulties under two categories, academic and social. Socially, Christy likes consistency and rules and can perform quite well once he knows what is expected from him. Social skills training had been considered to be important within his primary school, and this has supported him in making friends and getting involved in activities with his peers. However, similar to other children with Asperger syndrome (AS) he experiences anxiety when events happen out of context and unfamiliar demands are placed on him to relate or behave in a way that is not consistent for him. Academically, he has problems staying on task, concentrating, organizing himself and integrating information that is presented to him. In particular, he finds it quite difficult to get himself organized to do his homework. The development of his Individual Education Plan (IEP) had addressed some of these problems, and with the help of his resource and class teacher he manages to achieve what work is set for him. However, this work is carefully monitored so that it does not place undue anxiety on him and that he experiences success. One of the main concerns expressed by Christy's mother was that there would be a continuum of support within the post-primary school, including easy access to staff so that problems would not escalate before she had managed to speak to a teacher. Access to a 'significant adult' was also important for Christy so that he would have somebody to talk to and confide in should he be experiencing difficulties. Subject choice was seen as important as Christy had expressed a desire to do woodwork and his mother felt that this provided a calming effect for him within the school environment. Other problems like negotiating the school, locating lockers and classrooms, homework and bullying were highlighted as causing anxiety for both Christy and his mother.

After extensive investigations into various schools Christy's mother found a local school that had secured funding to set up a support class for first-year pupils with AS. The numbers are small at present (4). Christy and another boy are actually mainstreaming and access the support class for resource hours and teaching. A buddy system is in operation where Christy has access to a mentor – a current student to whom he can talk – and he also has access to a member of staff who will liaise with Christy and his parents by phone or by email should an issue occur. A special needs teacher and a year head complete the support system for pupils within the support class. Christy's mother reports that he has settled in better than they had anticipated. His locker is located in the support class to help alleviate problems, and he is organizing himself better than expected. He takes his laptop from class to class and so far is managing well to keep up with his peers, which has helped to ease his anxiety. He also, to their surprise, has taken up a language and is enjoying woodwork. He has not had any problems with bullying and is so tired each evening that he is sleeping well and is happy to go to school each day. If things get too much for him he can access the support class but to date he has not availed of this. The access for both Christy and his parents to staff has, in his mother's opinion, eased the transition process, and the efforts on behalf of the school to accommodate his needs have helped reduce the anxiety for all parties involved. In particular, lack of access had been highlighted as being a stumbling block by other parents (whose children did not have AS) and consequently became an important issue for this family. Christy's mother acknowledged that his primary school had done such a good job with him that she hoped moving schools would not set him back.

The triangulated system of support provided to Christy, his teachers and parents was considered by his mother to be crucial for the transition process and his well-being in post-primary school. While these experiences have helped to ease the transition process for Christy only time will tell as to whether he will remain and succeed in mainstream education as he also negotiates the biological, cognitive and emotional changes characteristic of adolescent development.

POST-SCHOOL TRANSITION

Systemic structures can facilitate or prevent appropriate transitions to post-school provision. The 'grey' area between children's and adult services was a source of deep frustration for parents and young people in England, Wales and Scotland:

> This is our next stumbling block to be honest. The thought of losing (that service) at the end of this year, before her 17th birthday was starting to panic me a bit and when you contact them it's like 'well it's not children's services now' so you go to adult services and they say 'oh but she's not 18 yet' so there's this bit between 16 and 18 that nobody wants to take ownership of and you're left thinking 'where do I go from here?' (Lewis, Parsons and Robertson 2007, p.96)

> Our main worries are for life beyond college. We would love (him) to have a fulfilling life but are not sure what is available for him, we would hate for him to be stuck in a Day Centre doing meaningless

activities. The worst thing is that you can't plan for it; you don't know what services will be available; don't know if (he) will qualify for the Independent Living Fund. It's about picking him up on the radar. Transition…is a big problem; communication between children and adult services is very scant. (Lewis *et al.* 2007, p.97)

School structures also can encourage or hinder the aspirations of young people with disabilities and/or special educational needs as they seek a pathway to a future career alongside their peers. Formal and informal school structures, including curricular access, social relationships and teacher expectations, can shape and influence the choices available to these young people: 'Where young people have disabilities and require additional support needs over their peers, the choices available to them, in relation to academic subjects and future careers may be severely truncated' (Shah 2005, p.112).

Young people with disabilities can adopt a fatalistic attitude as they believe they have little control over planning for a future after school (Mortimer 2004). One young person believed this was the reason underlying the decision to leave school early:

I suppose they would see that there would be limits on what they can do anyway, when they are older, so they don't see the need to get education, because they probably see that they won't be able to do a lot of jobs anyway. (Daly, Keogh and Whyte 2008, pp.28)

Teacher expectations are a critical factor in facilitating the realization of the aspirations of young people with disabilities and/or special educational needs. Negative teacher assumptions about the capacity of these young people to succeed has been reported, in particular for those who have dyslexia:

Some found it hard to believe that someone with dyslexia would want to go to college.

Join NCAD (National College of Art and Design) that is all you are good for.

Bad spelling in school they will crucify you in college.

(Kenny, McNeela and Shevlin 2001, p.6)

Young people with a physical disability may perceive that their special school lacked ambition for them and may see a disparity with their later experiences in education:

> It's not that I couldn't do them [exams], they just never gave me a chance to do them and I had seen other people doing exams and I thought, why can't I do them? Every time I asked them, it was like 'because' all the time. When I went to Pathfinders [support scheme in FE Colleges for disabled students], I put the emphasis on them that I want to do an exam in whatever and they said 'no problem, go for it', and I left there with GCSEs, so. (Educable 2000, pp.33–34)

Stereotypical attitudes about appropriate careers for young people with disabilities have also been reported:

> I was encouraged to do computers...obviously I cannot just walk into any job. Guidance teacher suggested computers.

> I always got – you should be a secretary.

> (Kenny et al. 2001, p.6)

However, enabling teachers recognize capacity and encourage young people to attempt to achieve their ambitions:

> We were not expected to go to college. Individual teachers did help me and knew my capabilities. (Kenny et al. 2001, p.7)

> I have a duty to change people's attitudes because there are people out there who think disability is a big horrible thing... My school was the place that if ever there was a burden it was lifted because they wanted me to succeed. (Daly et al. 2008, p.39)

In a very real sense young people with disabilities and/or special educational needs are asked to traverse two distinct worlds (disabled/non-disabled) and negotiate a pathway towards becoming an autonomous adult. This aspiration can be thwarted when there is a lack of knowledge and recognition that they, by virtue of receiving support for additional needs, can be consigned to a disabled path in life unless educators and policy makers actively challenge this outcome. Some teachers may be uncomfortable with an advocacy role; however, when we acknowledge the struggle of disabled people in overcoming negative expectations and assumptions, there is an onus on us as educators to promote positive expectations:

> Looking to expand the boundaries of life, I decided to sit the Leaving Certificate in our local post-primary school. To my amazement, my application was turned down on the basis that I might fail the examination and this would spoil their academic record... Having successfully completed my examination, I approached a disability

organisation for the first time seeking guidance for my next step. Eventually, the social worker recommended that I should take a job in a factory making brushes. My brief encounter with the 'disabled world' convinced me that I must make my own way.

This student successfully completed an honours Arts degree in university and, along with her peer group, approached the careers office to discuss career options:

> I was advised to be proud of my achievement, frame my certificate but not to expect a place in the world of work. It was evident that there were two tracks – two sets of expectations for people with and without disabilities. This dual reality still exists in the twenty first century. (O'Leary 2003, pp.277–278)

Active participation in all decision-making processes affecting their lives has to become the norm for these young people at all stages of their educational career. Expecting young people to make a valued contribution at 16 or 17 can be unrealistic if they have little experience of active participation in decision making to date. Effecting change in how disability is characterized within schools and society will require active listening by educators to the young people of concern. This dialogue can be the foundation for transition planning that recognizes the capabilities of these young people, and can indeed have a societal impact, as this discussion between three students (S1, S2 and S3) with disabilities shows:

> S1 Some people's disability can be shrouded in different ways. In today's world if you can't see it they assume 'he'll be able to do this', and you might not be able to.
>
> S2 It should be recognised more publicly, not only in education.
>
> S1 In the whole of society.
>
> S3 People don't understand, and you can't really expect them to either because there is nothing out there to tell them about this.
>
> S1 My county council is fully accessible and even have one member of staff in a wheelchair.
>
> S2 I think that's marvellous.
>
> S3 That shouldn't be looked on as that's brilliant. This should be an everyday thing and it should be ongoing as well.
>
> (Kenny et al. 2000, pp.46–77)

These young people envisaged that an advocate who had a disability could be a role model and spokesperson and help to transform expectations and assumptions concerning disabled people:

> He could be the spokesperson for people with disabilities, because some disabled people would be afraid to admit openly that they've a problem. People assume 'Oh God love him', and pity him. I think if someone was on a council… they would say 'listen if he's on the government, he's bright' and then naturally from the top it would go down very slowly to everywhere, and everyone would be offered jobs, disabled and able bodied working together in the same place and Ireland would become a better place to live in. (Kenny *et al.* 2000, p.50)

School life for children and young people with disabilities and/or special educational needs involves a series of intersecting organizational and learning transitions. Many of these children require structured support to make a successful transition within school and/or between schools. Educators need to ensure that this support enables the child/young person to 'have a real say' in the decision-making processes that profoundly affect their lives. Otherwise, there is a real risk that the support offered, while well intentioned, can further marginalize these young people and compromise their active participation in shaping their lives.

SUMMARY

In this chapter we have:

- examined how children and young people with disabilities and/or special educational needs can be active participants in decision-making processes that affect their lives
- explored how educators can facilitate the involvement of these young people in developing individual education planning
- considered the multi-faceted nature of transition (primary/secondary; secondary/post-school) and how the nature of the transition impacts on the lives of children and young people.

REFERENCES

Chedzoy, S.M. and Burden, R.L. (2005) 'Assessing student attitudes to primary–secondary school transfer.' *Research in Education 74*, 22–35.

Children and Young People's Unit (2001) *Learning to Listen. Core Principles for the Involvement of Children and Young People.* London: HMSO.

Children in Scotland (2006) *My Turn to Talk? The Participation of Looked After and Accommodated Children in Decision-Making Concerning Their Care.* Edinburgh: Scottish Executive Education Department.

Daly, F., Keogh, F. and Whyte, J. (2008) *The Experiences of Students with Physical Disabilities in Second Level Schools.* Dublin: National Disability Authority.

Department for Education and Skills (1994) *Special Educational Needs Code of Practice.* London: HMSO.

Department for Education and Skills (2001) *Special Educational Needs Code of Practice.* London: HMSO.

Department of Education and Science (2007) *Inclusion of Students with Special Educational Needs Post-Primary Guidelines.* Dublin: Stationery Office.

Downing, J. (2004) 'Communication Skills.' In F. Orelove, D. Sobsey and R. Silberman (eds) *Educating Children with Multiple Disabilities: A Collaborative Approach,* pp.529–561 (2nd edition). Baltimore, MD: Paul H. Brookes.

Educable (2000) *No Choice: No Chance: The Educational Experiences of Young People with Disabilities.* Belfast: Save the Children & Disability Action.

Evangelou, M., Taggart, B., Sylva, K., Melhuish, M., Sammons, P. and Siraj-Blatchford, I. (2008) *Effective Pre-school, Primary and Secondary Education 3–14 Project. What Makes a Successful Transition from Primary to Secondary School?* Research Report DCSF-RR019. Institute of Education, University of London.

Gross, J. (2000) 'Paper promises? Making the Code work for you.' *Support for Learning 15*, 3, 126–133.

Hamilton, M. (2009) 'Putting words in their mouths: the alignment of identities with system goals through the use of Individual Learning Plans.' *British Educational Research Journal 35*, 2, 221–242.

Kenny, M., McNeela, E., Shevlin, M. and Daly, T. (2000) *Hidden Voices: Young People with Disabilities Speak about Their Second Level Schooling.* Cork: South West Regional Authority.

Kenny, M., McNeela, E. and Shevlin, M. (2001) *Experiences of Students with Disabilities in Higher Education.* Dublin: Association for Higher Education Access & Disability (AHEAD). Unpublished Report.

Lewis, A., Parsons, S. and Robertson, C. (2007) *My School, My Family, My Life: Telling It Like It Is. A Study Detailing the Experiences of Disabled Children, Young People and Their Families in Great Britain in 2006.* University of Birmingham & Disability Rights Commission.

McCauley, E. (2009) 'Transition from primary to post-primary schools: issues for students with special educational needs.' *REACH (Journal of Special Needs Education in Ireland) 23*, 1, 32–46.

MacConville, R. (2007) *Looking at Inclusion: Listening to the Voices of Young People.* London: Paul Chapman.

Mortimer, H. (2004) 'Hearing children's voices in the early years.' *Support for Learning 19*, 4, 169–174.

National Council for Special Education (2006) *Guidelines on the Individual Education Plan Process.* Dublin: The Stationery Office.

O' Donnell, M. (2003) 'Transfer from Special to Mainstream: The Voice of the Pupil.' In M. Shevlin and R. Rose (eds) *Encouraging Voices: Respecting the Insights of Young People Who Have Been Marginalised,* pp.228–253. Dublin: National Disability Authority.

O'Leary, K. (2003) 'Living in the Real World.' In M. Shevlin and R. Rose (eds) *Encouraging Voices: Respecting the Insights of Young People Who Have Been Marginalised* (pp.277–279). Dublin: National Disability Authority.

Priestley, M. (1999) 'Discourse and Identity: Disabled Children in Mainstream High Schools.' In S. French and M. Corker (eds) *Disability Discourse* (pp.92–102). Buckingham: Open University Press.

Shah, S. (2005) 'Voices and choices: how education influences the career choices of young disabled people.' *Journal of Research in Special Educational Needs 5*, 3, 112–117.

Shier, H. (2001) 'Pathways to participation: openings, opportunities and obligations.' *Children & Society 15*, 2, 107–117.

Thomas, N. (2002) *Children, Family and the State: Decision Making and Child Participation.* London: The Policy Press.

Thompson, A., Morgan, C. and Urquhart, I. (2003). 'Children with ADHD transferring to secondary schools: potential difficulties and solutions.' *Clinical Child Psychology and Psychiatry 8*, 91–103.

Tod, J. (1999) 'IEPs: inclusive educational practices?' *Support for Learning 14*, 4, 184–188.

Tur-Kaspa, H. (2002) 'The socio-emotional adjustment of adolescents with learning disabilities in the Kibbutz during high school transition periods.' *Journal of Learning Disabilities 35*, 87–96.

Wearmouth, J. (2001) 'Inclusion – Changing the Variables.' In L. Peer and G. Reid (eds) *Dyslexia – Successful Inclusion in the Secondary School.* London: David Fulton.

West, P., Sweeting, H. and Young, R. (2008) 'Transition matters: pupils' experiences of the primary–secondary school transition in the West of Scotland and consequences for well-being and attainment.' *Research Papers in Education,* 1–29.

Woolfson, R., Harker, M., Lowe, D., Shields, M., Banks, M., Campbell, L. and Ferguson, E. (2006) 'Consulting about consulting: young people's views of consultation.' *Educational Psychology in Practice 22*, 4, 337–353.

CHAPTER 7

Children as Active Participants in the School Community

Within this chapter we will examine how schools, teachers and peers can facilitate a process of empowerment for children and young people who have disabilities and/or special educational needs. Key issues to be addressed include ensuring curricular access; supporting learning and social needs; enabling pupils to become more autonomous; and developing teacher skills in active listening and responding appropriately. We conclude the chapter with an in-depth case study that explores how a child with attention deficit hyperactivity disorder (ADHD) at risk of exclusion from school was enabled to participate actively in lessons and modify his behaviour.

Responding appropriately to the individual learning and social needs of children and young people with special educational needs requires a multi-level response from schools, teachers and peers. Consultation with and respect for rights of children and young people with special educational needs must be built into the whole fabric of the school and permeate school policy and practice. Schools that respond appropriately to individual needs appear to be characterized by a number of common features. These schools tended to have a tradition of catering for pupils with a wide range of individual needs.

Creating an appropriate learning environment for all pupils constitutes the first priority for any school, and with this in place more specialized individual needs can be addressed (Wilson 2004). Teachers have been seen to develop their pedagogy through focusing on learner needs rather than the presenting impairment, and to attempt to create appropriate learning opportunities based on an analysis of learner needs rather than presumptions about learning associated with particular impairments. In this way, children and young people with special educational needs can be enabled to challenge low expectations, inform teachers of their individual needs and express their views (McArthur *et al.* 2007).

We will here explore and document how schools, teachers, support staff and peers have responded proactively to the learning and social needs of children and young people with special educational needs. We will see how a school community can ensure curricular access; provide appropriate supports and foster autonomy; listen to and respond to the concerns of children and young people; and affirm their value and self-worth within the school.

ENSURING CURRICULAR ACCESS

Ensuring curricular access is a critical component of enabling children and young people with special educational needs actively to participate in school life. Facilitating curricular access is an essential prerequisite to involving these young people in decision-making processes around their education. Barriers to participation can be numerous and varied including inaccessible physical environments, unwarranted teacher assumptions about ability and consequent low expectations, support that encourages dependency and lack of peer group understanding. However, school and teacher engagement with the development of access routes involving the children and young people with special educational needs can address and overcome many of these barriers.

A number of studies (Kenny, McNeela and Shevlin 2003; Kenny *et al.* 2000; Lewis, Parsons and Robertson 2006; Lewis, Robertson and Parsons 2005; MacConville 2007) offer important insights into how children and young people with disabilities and/or special educational needs can be enabled to participate actively in decision-making processes around their education. These studies examined the educational barriers experienced by these young people and their families and explored ways of overcoming these barriers. It became evident that the young people were quite capable of identifying their educational and access needs and that they valued when teachers recognized their individual needs without having to be constantly reminded.

Facilitating the active participation of these pupils in school life involves multi-level strategies from schools ranging from whole-school approaches, awareness raising and fostering positive expectations among teachers and pupils.

Access to school is critical, and in so far as possible this process should resemble the ordinary process experienced by all children. Some described their access as relatively straightforward:

> It was nice being with the normal crowd. It was just around the corner and I liked it and I put my name down, that's how I got to go there.

> I thought it was a good school, it catered for disabled people and it had two resource teachers and if you needed help with any subject they'd give you special tuition on a one to basis. (Kenny *et al.* 2000, p.22)

In another school others reported that physical access was guaranteed:

> There were girls in wheelchairs and they got round easily and everything was at a level where they could do everything. (p.24)

As Kenny *et al.* commented: 'Flexibility in the built environment is possible and promoted access to activities. It is clear…that access to the built environment and to the academic process were often almost synonymous' (p.24).

A whole-school approach was documented in two schools where ensuring curricular access was not confined to the individual classroom teacher and/or support team, rather this was perceived as the responsibility of the school community (Lewis *et al.* 2005). These schools had developed ICT resources to support access needs including interactive whiteboards, voice amplification system and recordable 'button' devices to note a verbal response from a non-verbal pupil.

Facilitating the participation of young people in the classroom and the curriculum demands proactive interventions by the teacher. Teachers need actively to seek out pupil abilities and not assume their incompetence when tackling curricular tasks (MacConville 2007). Teachers also need to find ways to communicate with the pupil that are supportive rather than judgemental and allow sufficient time for pupils to express their views.

Teachers who recognize and respond to individual needs in a precisely targeted matter-of-fact way are particularly appreciated:

> I never had a problem with a teacher, they were all real nice… They knew I couldn't write fast and they encouraged me to use the typewriter, but it was too big to carry around so I didn't. When I went into the senior cycle they gave me a personal assistant. He took out the books and wrote down notes; he was just real nice. (Kenny *et al.* 2000, p.29)

The same research showed that supportive teachers accept a student's disability as no more or less than itself, and work with or around it and find ways to involve the student with a disability:

> ...some did their best to accommodate you with notes and extra time for essays to be handed up. (p.30)

Positive teacher responses also occur in the informal domain. A young person with dyslexia particularly treasured this support as it built up the pupil's skills, self-worth and ambition:

> ...a few teachers took me aside and went through things with me. But we had to work in the canteen; there was nowhere else. Classmates were astonished at me – spending time with a teacher! If they knew what they were talking about they'd know I needed the extra help. (p.30)

Guaranteeing that pupils have choice and flexibility in participation can be very helpful:

> [It's] about having the choice...we could have a GCSE Science scheme here and one in mainstream so some students if they wanted to go to a mainstream class they could but some who aren't sure could do GCSE Science here...where they feel more comfortable and if they want to do the integration scheme when they are more comfortable then they can. (Lewis *et al.* 2005, p.9)

Often schools appear to have difficulties ensuring that pupils with disabilities can participate in practical activities, such as physical education and science lessons. But this is not always the case:

I'm actually involved in the Rounders team and you would think 'a visually impaired child involved in Rounders, how can she even whack the ball?' They've got a special ball for me...so I can access a lot of stuff at school. (Lewis *et al.* 2006, p.76)

> I wasn't excluded from any sports. Actually they pushed me into things more than taking me out – 'you are going into this, no questions asked!' (Kenny *et al.* 2003, p.31)

> I'm involved in sport myself. If they were playing soccer or whatever I'd referee or something like that. No problem, I used love it. (Kenny *et al.* 2000, p.31)

Sometimes teachers employ peer support for a pupil with a physical disability to enable direct participation, in this case in a science lesson (Kenny *et al.* 2000):

> We'd pair up, and my partner used to do all the physical work. I just couldn't do it; I couldn't hold a glass of water. (p.31)

Another science teacher was prepared to let a pupil with a physical disability take an acceptable risk in participation and so allow him to learn:

> Doing science…I nearly burnt my hands a few times. I was allowed to again but I kept my eyes open more. (p.31)

Promoting involvement in extracurricular activities can be particularly beneficial and can give young people an opportunity to explore possibilities for self-development:

> My whole week I am doing stuff, lunchtimes and after school, English, maths, DT…*you know there's no limit to what you can do,* especially at lunchtime and after school. (Lewis et al. 2005, p.6) (bold italics in the original)

Some schools recognize that accessible transport could be an issue for pupils with physical disabilities in participating in extracurricular activities and have responded positively (Kenny *et al.* 2000):

> I went on a lot of trips. The other students had to make their own way; we got transport no problem from school. (p.32)

In another school in the same study including everyone in the school musical was the norm and the young person with a physical disability was no exception:

> Everybody had to do the school musical. I found I actually enjoyed it and it was one of the things I could be involved in. (p.32)

Enabling pupils to access examinations at their appropriate level can also be fraught with difficulties, though positive teacher reinforcement can be very effective:

> Today I got told I could do Art GCSE but other teachers have told me I'm not capable of doing Art GCSE and I go to another [mainstream] school today for integration and he says I'm well capable and I've got to do it and I'm feeling really proud and I'm like why is everyone telling me I can't do it? (Lewis *et al.* 2006, p.81)

Children with autism spectrum disorder (ASD) are particularly prone to being misunderstood by their teachers and peer group and also to their own misunderstanding of the social interactions that permeate the classroom (MacConville 2007). It is imperative that teachers take time to understand these children's perceptions and not immediately classify them as lazy, rude or naughty.

There appears to be evidence that the cognitive ability of children with dyslexia is consistently underestimated, and that the actual diagnosis can mark a turning point in the school career of these children. There is evidence that families can be reluctant to talk about disability/special educational needs with their children, a reluctance shared by some teachers. However, the official recognition of the learning difficulty can have a very positive impact on the child's self-perception as a learner (MacConville 2007). The difficulties experienced by the child can now be placed within a reasonable structure and more easily understood by teachers and attract appropriate support. Positive interventions where the child is encouraged and supported in tackling manageable tasks can increase the child's confidence in learning. It is also important to recognize that the child's strengths may lie in oral rather than written contributions, and this type of input needs to be valued in classroom interactions and assessments.

SUPPORT AND AUTONOMY

For many children with special educational needs the provision of appropriate support is essential to facilitate active participation in classroom activities and social inclusion within schools. However, 'there is a fine line between support that facilitates social inclusion and support that inhibits interaction and autonomy' (Egilson and Traustadottir 2009, p.33).

Children and young people who have special educational needs usually have high levels of interaction with adults in school compared to their peers and so often require the creation of opportunities to experience and act autonomously.

As schools and teachers often face the dilemma of how to offer adequate support for individual needs without compromising the child's independence and autonomy, the child's perspective can be a very useful indicator of the success or otherwise of school initiatives to promote autonomy. Schools can conceptualize and organize support that involves the active participation of pupils, and this involves checking with them regularly about their support needs, accepting their assessment of the value of the support and involving their friends in the process.

Pupils in one school reported that they did not feel stigmatized in receiving help which appeared to be 'an accepted normality for the pupils and the class' (Lewis *et al.* 2006, p.57). It seems that support, no matter how complex, can become the accepted norm:

> What might on first impression seem to be sophisticated and complicated equipment, highly personal forms of support, or unusual approaches to learning, became part of routine school arrangements. (Shaw 1998, p.75)

One young person who had a physical disability experienced the sense of freedom only when she went to college, as the assistive technology was not available in her school:

> I have the technology now which are my wings, that's the biggest difference. I can overcome people's attitudes now, I can, I'm independent, I can read on my own, I can type on my own. I haven't come up against exams yet so I will see how that goes. (Kenny *et al.* 2003, p.151)

In particular, pupils appear to value appropriate support and want to be listened to when individual needs are addressed. When pupils are actively involved in assessing their level of support they are enabled to be confident and assertive:

> Sometimes in practicals in Science, it's a little bit too much help. I can do things myself but they don't realise it so I actually have to tell them all. (Lewis *et al.* 2006, p.58)

One pupil in the same study was confident enough to assert herself when challenged:

> On one occasion an auxiliary told her that she should not be using a calculator and Tanya replied confidently, saying that it was OK with the teacher. (p.58)

And one parent observed that her daughter:

> is an intelligent girl who does not want to feel different; the [mainstream] school has managed to give her support without undermining her confidence. They have encouraged her ability to be autonomous; there has been no belittling of her. (p.47)

Schools need to adapt to changing circumstances. In this case an assistant to a child with a physical disability (Simon) left the school. Simon was enabled to take more responsibility for his access needs with positive results:

> Something happened after he was given the key to the elevator whereby he managed to get around school on his own. He is a totally different and far more independent person. (Egilson and Traustadottir 2009, p.30)

It appeared that this opportunity to act autonomously enabled him to become more integrated into social activities with his peer group who gave practical support:

> Originally, they (the boys) were just looking for something to do, I think. But now they find Simon fun to be with… They join him during recess and they run and turn around and I am just scared stiff. But it is all very enjoyable. (p.30)

Pupils often describe supportive teachers as caring and dependable and willing to consult the child about individual needs and offer appropriate responses:

> We were in Maths and my Maths teacher was a fantastic teacher. For a couple of months he let me be and then came up to me and said what would you like me to do to help you? I said you're doing brilliantly. (Lewis et al. 2006, p.158)

From the pupil perspective it is important that teachers check with them about their individual needs and preferences and offer appropriate support:

> I think if teachers are supportive and say look is there anything that you don't understand just ask or maybe stay behind the lesson if you've got a question and just make it clear that they can help you with whatever you are struggling with. (Lewis et al. 2006, p.106)

This point is reinforced by one pupil with emotional behavioural difficulties who had particularly benefited from sensitive nuanced support and as a result had an increased capacity to cope with the stresses and challenges of classroom interaction:

> I've improved a lot since I've had my helper. She was my friend. She wasn't just my teacher. She helped me to understand life. I can take it now. I don't get in a huff and a puff when people call me names, I don't run out of the class and hide or something like that. I tell my teacher or I sort it out myself. She helped me to understand why I

shouldn't be doing this or I should be doing that. She understands what I was going through so she knew how to stop it. (Shaw 1998, p.76)

One study explored the perceptions of pupils with hearing impairments about their experiences in mainstream school (Rooney 2003). These pupils were comfortable in approaching their teachers in relation to expressing their needs and requesting certain practical arrangements, such as asking the teachers to speak slowly and clearly in the class situation:

> They're very helpful, if I don't understand what they are talking about, they'll stay behind with me after class and they'll explain it to me rather than rushing through it myself afterwards. And sometimes, I come into school early the following day, around 8.30am and explain it in more detail. (p.164)

Generally, these pupils felt that their class teachers expected them to perform as well as their hearing peers. The majority of them maintained that once they used their technical aids, such as the hearing and the radio-aids, and took ownership for their work, they were equal to and as capable as their hearing peers.

> I'm no different from other students in my class, so I don't think they expect anything less. (p.165)

Moreover, they strongly felt that this was reflected in the teachers' expectations of them in so far as they related to these pupils with the same respect as they would with the hearing students:

> Basically, I try to be independent as I can and I don't go out of my way to, you know, make it all, you know 'look at me, I have a hearing aid so treat me different,' and I think they respect me for that as well, which is a good thing. (pp.165-166)

It appears that pupils do not generally want to be treated as special cases and appreciate sensitive respectful approaches from teachers:

> I trust the staff here, the way they act towards you. You can have a laugh with them in lessons and they don't mind you walking around with them while they are doing their duties at lunchtime, it's not like 'Oh I can't be bothered now'. (Lewis *et al.* 2005, p.15)

While aware of differences in attitudes towards them, some pupils wanted to be treated the same as others (Lewis *et al.* 2006):

> I'd rather be treated the same. I think everybody wants to be treated the same basically. It's nice to have the attention occasionally but when it comes down to it you all want to be part of the pack don't you? (p.101)

Here friends were a valuable source of support for pupils, and this support could be informal:

> For example, I was kind of falling behind, and a friend…he helped, pushed me and I really appreciated that. (p.59)

Another pupil suggested that a peer mentoring programme organized by older pupils with experience of special educational needs would be very helpful in supporting other pupils who were beginning to adjust to having difficulties:

> There's got to be student involvement in it, because if you have a lot of people from higher up dictating how support is going to be offered then you could end up with an unresponsive system, you could work peer mentoring into that as well, including students from the start, maybe students who found out when they were six, and known for a lot longer…can support newly 'labelled' students into the society with dyslexic students, if they have the chance, mould themselves into, like a little protective group! (p.59)

ACTIVE LISTENING AND RESPONDING

School and teacher views on children and young people with special educational needs are often narrowly conceptualized in terms of their difficulties in learning and/or access needs. As a result, the capacity of these children to examine and reflect on their learning experiences can be seriously underestimated. Current childhood research has shown that: 'primary pupils are actually quite capable of reflecting upon their performance and behaviour in school and, given a supportive and enabling context, articulating this self-knowledge to others' (Ravet 2007, p.9).

One 14-year-old pupil with a physical disability advocated the consultation approach with pupils quite forcefully:

> Yeah, people will learn – it's good. People don't ask their opinions because they think they're thick, they're not though. It's a brilliant idea; it'll make life a lot better if they did, to facilitate them and all that. (O'Donnell 2003, p.247)

In Case study 7.1 the value of pupil consultation in effecting change is amply illustrated.

Case study 7.1 Thomas: supporting active participation

Thomas is a pupil with Asperger syndrome who attends a secondary school. He is well able to reflect upon his schooling experiences. The school has developed a policy of support that enhances his ability to interact socially and achieve academic success.

> She [the learning support assistant (LSA)] taught me how to understand the ways in which my Asperger's will affect me in my school life. We made a personal profile on 'PowerPoint' then she used it to train the teachers and it helped them to understand me. This has made things a lot better. We're going to do this every year so that I can reflect back on how I've changed.

Difficulties with social interaction experienced by Thomas are recognized and responded to appropriately:

> When I had difficulty joining in with others in Year 7, she worked with me and taught me how to do it.

Support for Thomas is sensitive, nuanced, tailored to his needs and his capacity for autonomy enhanced:

> I know I've made good progress because in junior school my support worker was always beside me in class. I love being the same as everyone else now. The LSAs give me more space in this school and the help I get is not forced on me any more.

Thomas believes that his confidence has increased with the certainty that when he needs help, academic or otherwise, this is forthcoming:

> At my school I would definitely get help with work such as planning and good content… My teachers want the best for me and they encourage me.

As a result, Thomas is able to reflect on how his situation in school has improved through encouraging and supporting his active participation:

> Before I knew I had Asperger's my junior schoolteachers thought I was a bad boy. The other children teased and bullied me and it was a horrible time. Now I am more confident because more people understand me…it's definitely getting better because more people take me as I am. That's because they have learned about me and

know what to do for the best and probably most important I am in a good school.

Thomas knows that his difficulties will be responded to appropriately and that he will be treated fairly and as a result is able confidently to assert his right to equal treatment:

I don't think I should be treated any different because I have Asperger's syndrome.

It is evident that Thomas and his LSA, who plays a critical role in enabling him to be an active participant in all aspects of school life, have established a trusting relationship and that Thomas's perspective on his condition has been incorporated and embedded into school understanding and consequent practice.

An illuminating example of how pupil disengagement can be re-conceptualized and how pupil voice can be incorporated into understanding this disengagement has been given by Jackie Ravet, a lecturer in the School of Education at the University of Aberdeen (Ravet 2007). Disengagement is viewed as a survival strategy by children and Ravet remarks that overcoming disengagement 'requires an authentic collaboration between pupils, teachers and parents in which survival strategies can be identified, addressed and replaced with more constructive and lasting forms of coping' (Ravet 2007, p.xiii).

Pupil misbehaviour or pupil disengagement as characterized by Ravet (2007) often generates a series of negative teacher reactions that in turn leads to more extreme behaviour, classroom disruption and the real possibility of pupil exclusion from school. She argues very cogently that the child deficit model of understanding pupil disengagement is unhelpful. Attributing misbehaviour solely to child and family factors misses the point and ignores the impact of contextual factors such as teachers, curriculum and peer relationships on pupil behaviour. Ravet asserts that schools and teachers need to re-conceptualize the meaning of disengagement and realize that:

classroom behaviour does not happen in a vacuum but is situated within an interpersonal classroom context. Thus making sense of disengagement means, in part, making sense of the environmental and relational factors that may be causing or perpetuating disengagement, and implies an acceptance of the possible influence, among other things, of the teacher, their teaching and the curriculum. (p.108)

From the pupil perspective, Ravet found that explanations for disengagement focused on the context factors for learning and pupils cited problems accessing the curriculum and writing exercises as a source of resentment. These pupils reported enjoying more active engagement with learning as in physical education and music lessons and found writing and mathematics difficult. They attributed their inclination to give up easily to context factors such as pace and volume of work and difficulties with the extent of tasks and producing ideas.

These pupils described their perceptions of themselves as learners and provided explanations for their disengaged behaviour. This behaviour, according to the pupils, served the dual purpose of escaping from uncomfortable learning situations and ensured a 'time-out' from classroom activities. These pupils also tended to have very negative emotions towards learning and mentioned feelings such as anger, fear, hatred, boredom and tiredness. Ravet was struck by the sheer intensity of the negative emotional experiences of the children and 'their inability, or unwillingness, to cast negative emotions aside in order to focus on academic tasks' (p.52).

Taking these negative emotions towards learning into account can be very difficult for teachers as the prevailing school culture appears to favour the putting aside of distractions and focusing on academic tasks. It appears that unless these negative emotions are addressed then little learning and much disruption will occur. Teaching emotional literacy needs to be a key component of any intervention strategy to support the learning of disengaged pupils.

One teacher in Ravet's study recognized the importance of addressing the emotional well-being of the pupils as an intrinsic element in the teaching and learning process 'by specifically involving them in discussions about their feelings and perceptions,' and this was linked to concrete strategies to engage the pupils in learning such as problem-solving activities 'that enabled them to identify and confront their difficulties' (p.30). Pupils were also actively involved in developing strategies to assess their own learning progress and outcomes.

EMPOWERMENT

Children and young people who have special educational needs often experience considerable stress in coping with difficult learning environments. Stress has multiple causes, including coping with academic challenges, and as children entered adolescence there were added pressures to engage with peers and the outside world. One young person contrasted her experiences in primary and post-primary education:

In primary you were to a certain degree protected by your parents. In second level it was just get the academic first, to be the same as everyone else. Then it started to be the stress – to stop being different, in social life and academic. (Kenny *et al.* 2000, p.43)

Another young person in the same study concurred with this view:

Even if you improved the teachers and everything you do have more stress. Maybe not from school – it comes from other aspects, the social aspect is hard enough. (p.43)

The pressures of coping with school challenges appeared to result in some pupils in this study limiting both their social lives and opportunities for peer interaction:

I definitely was stressed out. I didn't go out socialising at weekends; life was on hold for at least three years. I had to do well to get out of school and get on in life, so it was head down. (p.43)

I didn't get involved at all in anything because I was always trying to survive. Get through school. I suppose confidence-wise I just dropped because of the general attitude. I went into a world of my own and I didn't bother, I couldn't mix with people I couldn't. (p.41)

The coping mechanism for another pupil involved reaching inside himself for solutions and getting the difficulty into perspective:

You do figure out ways to cope with it. If you deal with it inside yourself you win half the battle. The other half is to just open and admit you have a little bit of a problem. The only person it will affect is the one who has it, and the only way to cure it is to say 'right, what is your problem?' and narrow it down. When you narrow it down you can actually solve a lot of your problems. (p.43)

In developing appropriate responses for children and young people who have special educational needs, schools and teachers need to take account of the additional stress often experienced by these pupils. So, an empowering teacher is particularly appreciated by children and young people who have special educational needs: 'You need teachers that will keep you going and cheer you on' (Shaw 1998, p.80). Pupils particularly welcome teachers who see past their difficulties to the whole person, and encourage them to take risks:

One teacher kept driving me the whole way. Kind of 'put it in a context, fair enough you have a disability but – throw it away from

you and continue on' like. From that day on I've never looked back.
It was the best thing ever that, to stand up for ourselves. (Kenny *et al.*
2000, p.28)

Other teachers certainly empowered the next speaker, whose spirit had been
crushed by school and teacher responses to her undiagnosed dyslexia:

> I had two brilliant teachers, the career guidance and the history
> teacher. One fought for the special considerations for me for the
> Leaving Cert... I got into college through writing letters to them
> for three years. I didn't even get the points, I got it on pure annoying
> them too much — I think they were afraid to say no!... [The career
> guidance teacher] wrote to the Department of Education for three
> years. I stuck with the colleges, he stuck with the Department... He
> was an angel. (p.35).

One young person on the margins of the educational community was
encouraged to remain in school through the proactive response of the
teacher:

> When I first came here, I had given up on school altogether. I had got
> more and more behind with my workload and course work and I had
> got to the point where I thought I could do nothing. But when I got
> into school here, my teacher and I started planning. (Jelly, Fuller and
> Byers 2000, p.95)

Another school empowered a child who has brittle bone condition through
actively involving her in the recruitment of the child's support assistant
through writing the job description:

> Person must not want job for power. Person must be able to listen to
> child. Person must understand limits of safety. Person must be able to
> help friendships. Person must be strong and able to lift. Person must
> not get ill regularly. Person must listen to my Mummy. (Shaw 1998,
> p.78)

Case study 7.2 explores an intervention programme for a child who has
ADHD and was at serious risk of exclusion from school due to his aggressive
behaviour.

Case study 7.2 Alex: moving from isolation to participation

When I met 11-year-old Alex for the first time in October, his attitude
towards school and particularly his main teacher was very negative.
Further discussion elicited aggressive language and reaction, but most

apparent was a consistently hurt and depressed tone when chatting about every matter related to school and learning. My immediate concern at that time was a forthcoming school conference meeting planned for early November, at which Alex's increasingly challenging behaviour would be discussed, with the possibility of exclusion being one option on the agenda for consideration. His parents had asked me to talk to Alex and had obtained permission for me to attend the school meeting.

Compiling the background to date from everything he and his parents told me and from subsequent discussions with teachers from his school, I learned that Alex had been diagnosed with ADHD following psychological assessment when he was three years old and had been prescribed Ritalin, 30 mg daily. From preschool through to age 10–11 in primary school, Alex's behaviour had been sporadically aggressive and volatile, but it was agreed that with every new year in school he had become increasingly more difficult and his behaviour more challenging. Alex's primary concern when I met him first was that in his final year in primary school he had a new teacher, who was also new to the school. In his opinion they had clashed from the outset, which had culminated in particularly aggressive behaviour from him towards her, including name-calling and writing a number of distressing and angry notes to her. All of this had led to the planned school conference meeting where it was agreed to pursue alternative strategies rather than exclusion to help Alex overcome his difficulties in school, which included allowing me to become involved in this process by offering support both to Alex and his teacher as we pursued solutions that might help him engage more positively in the school environment.

Over the course of a number of meetings with Alex and his teacher between November and the Christmas holidays, and also as a result of my own observations of him in class, we each identified areas where Alex appeared to have particular difficulties that had led to aggressive outbursts or confrontation between Alex and his peers or Alex and his teacher. Interestingly, each of us had noted the same issues but, not surprisingly, Alex had the greatest insight into why these particular situations had arisen. Alex's teacher was struck by the fact that Alex was very quick to point out examples of his own challenging behaviour, but she was astounded when she realized that quite often some precipitative action or situation that she was not aware of had arisen first. In most cases, and to varying degrees, the identified trigger for outbursts or confrontations was frustration:

- because he hadn't understood an instruction fully
- because he felt he wasn't being listened to
- because he was conscious of his own lack of organizational skills

- because he had achieved something or done something well but nobody had noticed.

Initially, Alex and I discussed specific examples of the frustration he felt, and the most resounding image I got from this discussion was how exhausting it was for him to feel the way he did, especially when he was angry or got into trouble or confrontation. He wrote out suggestions as to what he felt he could do and what he thought his teacher could do to help both of them avoid these situations. One of his most interesting suggestions was that she find a way to make timed exercises easier for him. He invariably found that when his class were given specific short periods to complete an exercise or task, he would still be thinking about what he had to do when the others had finished and time was up. His teacher and I discussed this and decided to use an egg timer placed near him as his own personal timekeeping device. His teacher began changing the timed activities into multiples of three minutes to accommodate this experiment, and to her astonishment Alex wholeheartedly engaged with it and found that this tangible device helped him both to stay on task and to complete it on time. We concluded that this visual aid was more appealing than the face of the clock on the wall, but it was also important not to underestimate the satisfaction he felt when he realized that this experiment was as a direct result of his own suggestion and concern. Alex, quite evidently, was empowered by the fact that his identification of a problem had led to this solution.

Alex had also identified his own difficulties with organization, which constantly led to reprimands from and arguments with his main teacher and his learning support teacher who he worked with for half an hour every day. In order to help him with this and also to provide opportunity for positive behaviour acknowledgment, we created a sheet with Alex as a daily checklist to complete with his learning support teacher which included:

- punctuality
- homework
- materials
- attention
- new learning.

Each day they ticked the boxes to indicate the efforts he was making to arrive on time with the specific books and materials he needed for the different lessons, with his homework completed from the previous day and with a positive effort to pay attention and learn something new. If he didn't succeed in any or all, the experiment dictated that he wasn't reprimanded but simply the sheet wouldn't include a tick in the appropriate box or boxes. To begin with, a reward system was offered in which he chose an activity that he and his learning support teacher would concentrate on for the second half of their Friday class. Alex was very excited about the daily checklist and, as we monitored them over a period of three weeks coming up to the school break for Christmas, there was a very obvious improvement in the number of ticks on the daily sheets. Interestingly, the sheets were used from the beginning of the new term in January until Easter without any rewards on offer, but Alex continued to make consistent efforts to keep up the standards on the checklist. In the final term of school, the checklists were completed on a weekly basis rather than daily, and both Alex and his learning support teacher agreed that the excellent efforts he had been making in the previous term had been maintained.

Alex and I sat down with his teacher in February to review his progress to date and to discuss any further interventions that everyone might agree on. He explained to us how sometimes he could feel a burning sensation rising from his tummy to his head and that when this happened he wanted to throw something or kick something very hard. Both Alex and his teacher agreed that when he felt this happening to him, he should signal to his teacher by putting his hand up and turning it in a specific fashion so that she would understand how he was feeling. Her reaction to that would always be to give Alex a task involving him leaving the classroom for a few minutes. These tasks varied from carrying a note to either the learning support teacher or the vice-principal, who would allow him to spend some time in her room until he felt calmer or bring him for a walk or to the gym hall if it was unoccupied until he was ready to rejoin his class. Everyone involved in this intervention, including Alex, reported to me in May that this had proved to be very successful with fewer incidents of confrontation or inappropriate behaviour in class as a result.

The last intervention was very simple but particularly important to Alex. When I had met him first, he was very negative about school and believed that nobody liked him, including his classmates. There was only one boy in the class he was friendly with and he had made the point that he always felt a bit lost and more vulnerable whenever this boy wasn't reasonably close at hand. I discovered that the teacher had a policy of changing the pupils' seating arrangements on a monthly basis. As the pupils sat in groups of six, it was agreed that the two boys would always sit within the same group although in different seats. This simple plan seemed to give Alex renewed confidence and, as it was managed very discreetly, remained unobserved or noticed by any of his peers, including Alex's friend himself.

To conclude, I conducted final interviews with Alex and his teacher in June in which both were adamant that the school year had turned out to be much better than either had anticipated in October/November. The teacher had felt quite intimidated by Alex earlier in the year but confessed that once she had the opportunity to get to know him, that situation had changed completely. Instead she felt that she owed the child a debt of gratitude for showing her how to help him in the classroom. She also made the point that having the opportunity to discuss her concerns and worries, and then to analyse and track the impact of interventions, had boosted her confidence. Alex's parents, the learning support teacher and the vice-principal all agreed that what had begun as a rather destructive relationship between teacher and student had turned into a very positive one for both. Alex agreed with this assessment and told me that it had been a very good school year. He reported that his confidence and optimism had grown as a result of his involvement in devising strategies to help him manage his own behaviour and learning.

This case study reveals that with a supportive team Alex was enabled to become a full member of the class community and manage his own behaviour. Ultimately, Alex was the primary agent of change within his own environment, which helped him to move from a position of isolation as perceived by him, to one of participation and responsibility.

SUMMARY

In this chapter we have:

- considered how pupils with disabilities and/or special educational needs can be enabled to achieve curricular access
- explored how support for learning can be offered without compromising the autonomy of the child/young person
- considered how this often marginalized group of pupils can be encouraged to become active participants in the school community
- examined how active teacher listening and responding appropriately can enable pupils with special educational needs to become more confident and feel valued within the school environment.

REFERENCES

Egilson, S.T. and Traustadottir, R. (2009) 'Assistance to pupils with physical disabilities in regular schools: promoting inclusion or creating dependency?' *European Journal of Special Needs Education* 24, 1, 21–36.

Jelly, M., Fuller, A. and Byers, R. (2000) *Involving Pupils in Practice: Promoting Partnerships with Pupils with Special Educational Needs.* London: David Fulton.

Kenny, M., McNeela, E. and Shevlin, M. (2003) 'Living and Learning: The School Experiences of Some Young People with Disabilities.' In M. Shevlin and R. Rose (eds) *Encouraging Voices: Respecting the Insights of Young People Who Have Been Marginalised* (pp.138–158). Dublin: National Disability Authority.

Kenny, M., McNeela, E., Shevlin, M. and Daly, T. (2000) *Hidden Voices: Young People with Disabilities Speak about Their Second Level Schooling.* Cork: South West Regional Authority.

Lewis, A., Parsons, S. and Robertson, C. (2006) *My School, My Family, My Life: Telling It Like It Is. A Study Detailing the Experiences of Disabled Children, Young People and Their Families in Great Britain in 2006.* University of Birmingham & Disability Rights Commission.

Lewis, A., Robertson, C. and Parsons, S. (2005) *Experiences of Disabled Students and Their Families.* Phase 1 Research Report to Disability Rights Commission, June 2005. Birmingham: University of Birmingham, School of Education.

McArthur, J., Sharp, S., Kelly, B. and Gaffney, M. (2007) 'Disabled children negotiating school life: agency, difference and teaching practice.' *International Journal of Children's Rights 15,* 1–22.

MacConville, R. (2007) *Looking at Inclusion: Listening to the Voices of Young People.* London: Paul Chapman.

O'Donnell, M. (2003) 'Transfer from Special to Mainstream: The Voice of the Pupil.' In M. Shevlin and R. Rose (eds) *Encouraging Voices: Respecting the Insights of Young People Who Have Been Marginalized* (pp.228–253). Dublin: National Disability Authority.

Ravet, J. (2007) *Are We Listening? Making Sense of Classroom Behaviour with Pupils and Parents.* Stoke on Trent: Trentham Books.

Rooney, N. (2003) 'Creating a Culture of Change: Exploring the Perspectives of Young People with Hearing Impairments.' In M. Shevlin and R. Rose (eds) *Encouraging Voices: Respecting the Insights of Young People Who Have Been Marginalised* (pp.159–177). Dublin: National Disability Authority.

Shaw, L. (1998) 'Children's Experiences of School.' In C. Robinson and K. Stalker (eds) *Growing Up with Disability.* London: Jessica Kingsley Publishers.

Wilson, L.M. (2004) 'Towards equality: the voices of young disabled people in Disability Rights Commission research.' *Support for Learning 9,* 4, 162–168.

CHAPTER 8

Looking Ahead: Helping to Shape the Future of Student Involvement

Whilst there is increasing evidence of a willingness on the part of teachers and other professionals to involve young people in decision-making processes about their own lives, it is equally clear that a need to understand further how this might best be achieved remains.

Teachers generally know their pupils well and are best placed to put into action those approaches and changes that we have discussed in this book. If progress is to be made in fostering good teacher and pupil relationships built upon effective learning partnerships, it will be achieved through the actions of teachers keen to investigate their own practice and the impact of their approaches to teaching on the achievements of their pupils. As reflective practitioners, teachers have been leaders in educational change for as long as schools have existed.

In the area of pupil involvement, those innovations that we have witnessed in schools have come about as a result of the actions of teachers rather than through legislation. The search for more effective approaches to teaching and learning continues as a stimulus for teachers and researchers committed to school improvement. In this final chapter we will examine some of the ways in which teachers are currently exploring this area and raise issues which we believe would benefit from further investigation by classroom practitioners.

The notion that pupil involvement is an important area for further development cannot be doubted. Indeed the challenge of promoting pupil involvement has, in recent years, been brought sharply into focus as a result of a number of tragic incidents involving children and young people. In his report *The Protection of Children in England* Lord Laming (2009) emphasized the need to listen to young people in order to gain a better understanding of their lives and experiences. Lord Laming, in making recommendations for changes in procedures to improve child protection, recognized the importance of a children's work force skilled in eliciting information from young people about their own situation in order to afford a greater degree of care and support for children in difficulties.

Bob Reitemeier, Chief Executive of the Children's Society, a leading organization which advocates on behalf of children and their families, in a letter to Lord Laming at the outset of his inquiry observed:

> In our consultations with children and young people on the ECM [Every Child Matters] outcomes, two additional outcomes were suggested: one was being treated equally and the other was being listened to and taken seriously. We believe that the lack of attention to children and young people's views and experiences is the most significant barrier to good safeguarding practice and that it requires a real cultural shift, and not only professionally to effect the necessary change. (Reitemeier 2008)

The implications here that young people may at times be listened to but are not always taken seriously should be of concern to everyone working in services for children. Progress has certainly been made in providing opportunities for young people to voice their opinions, express their needs or request support in the context of both school and in-care provision. However, the impact of these procedures put into place in many instances through legislation can only be judged as successful where it is possible to see how children have influenced change. Many young people continue to believe that apparent efforts to seek their views remain at a tokenistic level and are conducted as a sop rather than with the sincerity they desire.

Throughout this book we have attempted to provide real-life examples of teachers encouraging pupils to become more engaged with the management of their own learning. Our motivations have largely centred upon a belief that as teachers we can learn more about how to become effective at our craft if we listen to what our pupils have to say about their experiences and how they see themselves as learners.

In conducting this work we have been acutely aware of the challenges that persist in working in this way. As with much learning, we have discovered that the more we learn about how to encourage pupils to take responsibility for some of their own education by being involved in processes of assessment and planning, the more aware we have become of the complexities of the issue. A number of obstacles present themselves to the teacher who is committed to ensuring that pupils have an opportunity to express their ideas and thereby gain greater insights into their own learning needs. We have therefore embarked upon this chapter with an intention of highlighting opportunities for systematic classroom-based inquiry and research into how we may move the agenda forward in respect of pupil involvement.

The word 'research' can at times appear problematic to teachers in schools, who may believe that research is the function of academics in universities and as such remains at a distance from their own practice. Such a notion, which has at times been perpetuated by an academic elite, is, we would suggest, an obstacle that can serve only to prevent a greater understanding of what works in our classrooms. It is our contention that educational research at its best starts from the questions that skilled teachers ask about their own practice with a clear intention to improve teaching and enhance the learning experiences of pupils.

The area of pupil involvement is ripe for further inquiry. It is evident that where teachers have applied the principles that support increased pupil autonomy in learning, they report successful outcomes and increased pupil engagement. However, much of what has been reported remains anecdotal and would benefit from verification through increased teacher research. Teachers are in a unique and privileged position in having opportunities to develop professional relationships with the pupils in their class and to gain daily insights into their achievements and the difficulties they may sometimes experience with learning.

By adopting a systematic approach to investigating pupil responses to classroom practices, teachers may change their practices and benefit their own teaching and the learning of their pupils. This does not require the development of elaborate research methods, but does require that teachers reflect upon their work and ask critical questions.

Case study 8.1 David: evaluating self-evaluation

David teaches a class of 10- and 11-year-old pupils in a primary school. For the past 18 months he has been encouraging his pupils to assess their own progress, identify their learning needs and set personal targets in their maths lessons. The pupils appear to enjoy being involved in this way, but David is keen to discover whether this is only his opinion, and to determine if the pupils believe that there are benefits in this approach to learning.

David's approach to maths teaching has been to encourage his pupils to evaluate what they have learned by first using an evaluation form, and then using this for the basis of a discussion with groups of pupils. His evaluation form has followed a set format, an example of which is given here:

Over the past four weeks we have been learning about decimals

We have used calculators to make calculations like $47.26 + 31.53 = 78.79$

We have also done these calculations without using calculators

We have worked out how to write decimals as fractions such as $7.25 = 7\ \frac{1}{4}$

How well have you understood the work that we have done?

☺	☺	☹
Very well	Quite well	Not very well

How much have you enjoyed the maths lessons during the past four weeks?

☺	☺	☹
A lot	They've been all right	Not very much

Are there things we have
done in maths lessons
that we need to practise
more?

After the pupils have filled in their evaluations he sits with them and talks to them about their responses. On the basis of this and combining the information with his own assessments of pupil performance he considers how effective he feels his teaching has been, and how well the pupils have met his lesson objectives.

David's concern is that having followed this procedure for the past 18 months, although the pupils are confident in conducting this form of self-evaluation, it may not be having the impact upon their learning that he wished for at the start of this process. His intentions had been to encourage the class to focus upon their own learning needs, to recognize their strengths and weaknesses and to provide him with feedback in relation to his teaching. He is now keen to establish whether these objectives have been met.

In order to investigate the impact of the procedures which he has developed David decides to go back through the evaluation forms he has collected during the past year and to ask the pupils to comment on whether they are now more confident about the learning that they indicated might need more attention. David sits with individuals and discusses with them the progress that they have made and what helped them to move forward. The following is an extract from one of David's interviews with one of his pupils.

David: Sometimes I ask everyone in the class to do an evaluation form for the work that we have been doing. Why do you think I do this?

Lucy: Because you want to know if we can do the work?

David: Yes, that's right. Are there any other reasons?

Lucy: Well, it makes us think a bit about what we have been doing and whether the work is easy or hard.

David: Good. Anything else?

Lucy: Well, if the work is hard, you give us some help so that we might find it easier to do.

David: Lucy, do you remember when you did your evaluation after the work we did on decimals? You said that you found it hard to understand how to convert decimals into fractions.

Lucy: I remember. I think some others in the class couldn't do it either.

David: Yes that's right. How do you feel about doing that maths now?

Lucy: I think I still sometimes make mistakes, but it's better than it was. I can do the work now but it still takes me longer than for some of the others in the class.

David: I don't think that it matters that you take longer. It's not a race. The important thing is that you understand and can do the work.

Lucy: I can do the decimals and fractions now. It's still hard sometimes but better than before.

David: What helped to make it better for you?

Lucy: I think the games we played were good.

David: Which games were those?

Lucy: You remember. The games you gave to me and Kevin. The ones we used to play when we first came in in the mornings.

David: Ah yes, now I remember. The decimals and fractions card game I gave you to play. Is that what you mean?

Lucy: Yes, that's right, those cards. Kevin and me, we played it every morning when we came in.

David: And that helped you to get better at the work?

Lucy: Of course it did.

David: Can we look at your evaluation form together, the one you filled in after we had done the decimals work? If you look here, you told me that you didn't understand the work very well, although you also said that maths lessons had been all right. If you were going to fill in the form now, what would you tell me?

Lucy: About the decimals?

David: Yes, how do you feel about doing this work now?

Lucy: I think I would say quite well. I can do the sums quite well, but still not very well.

David: Okay, so you have clearly learned about doing this work and you are doing better than before? Is that right?

Lucy: Yes.

David: So did the evaluation help? Do you think doing the evaluation was a good thing?

Lucy: Yes.

David: Why do you think it was a good thing?

Lucy: Well, I suppose it lets me tell you when I think I'm not very good at something.

David: How does that help?

Lucy: Well, when I tell you I'm not very good at things, you help me more. Like the game for me and Kevin. That really helped.

David is reassured that Lucy is able to indicate the value of the self-evaluation system he has put into place. He also feels that there is some indication here that the system is having an impact upon pupils' learning as a result of his own actions following the evaluations.

In Case study 8.1 David was obviously interested to know whether Lucy was gaining in confidence in mathematics lessons. However, he was equally concerned to know what she felt about the value of the self-evaluation procedures he had implemented in the classroom. This type of reflective approach, in which the teacher makes a reappraisal of an initiative, is important in schools where the staff are concerned to ensure that teaching and learning are being effectively managed. David is concerned to develop his own skills as a teacher and to implement procedures that help him to inquire into the impact of his work in the class. Furthermore, he recognizes that this may best be achieved by involving his pupils in this form of reflective practice. David believes that his pupils can provide a unique insight into his teaching and that by listening to what they say he may be able to learn more about himself as a teacher and modify his performance for the benefit of all pupils.

At the outset of this chapter we established our intention to set out a research agenda in the area of pupil involvement. Some teachers may well regard the example given in the case study above as simply an example of good teaching practice. It may be the case that some teachers would not regard this kind of reflective behaviour as having more than a tenuous relationship to research. We would contend, however, that the term *research* has often been viewed as an elite activity undertaken by academics and requiring formal procedures in order to yield data that might be of value. This concept of research needs to be challenged. Whilst there will always be a place for the large-scale formal educational research project, classroom practice in individual schools is as likely to be changed as a result of small-scale investigations into teaching and learning as it may be from larger-scale studies. However, if reflective classroom practice is to have an impact, it needs to be both systematic and founded upon approaches that will provide a genuine opportunity to question and challenge existing practices. Teachers need to gather evidence about their own teaching and the learning of their pupils in order to be able to effect change in the classroom (Cordingley 2004). A process whereby teachers implement teaching initiatives, formulate questions and gather evidence about their effectiveness and modify their actions as a result of this can legitimately be described as a research process. Furthermore, this form of systematic inquiry can be influential in changing classroom and school cultures and encouraging the development of an increasingly skilled teaching profession (Loughran 1999).

Teachers need to adopt a set of principles that will enable them to focus upon learning from within their classrooms and to develop a systematic approach to classroom inquiry. The time teachers currently have to reflect upon the work they undertake is limited by their busy schedules and the everyday demands made upon them. For this reason, if researching into their own work is perceived to be an addition to their workload, it is unlikely that it will ever become the priority it could, and we would suggest should, be.

As teachers, we all know of pupils who struggle with learning. We have all encountered learners who don't engage effectively with the teaching materials to which others appear so readily to respond. We similarly recognize those pupils who show their frustration with learning through adverse behaviour or disengagement with their work. Throughout this book we have attempted to demonstrate how, by putting pupils at the heart of the assessment, planning and evaluation of their own learning, we may begin to address some of the challenges both they and their teachers face every day in their classrooms. It is our belief that by setting an agenda for researching the procedures described in this book, which also calls upon the full involvement of pupils, we may learn more about effective teaching and thereby improve classroom practices for all parties. In order to achieve this, we would suggest that the following principles are important.

- When pupils evaluate their own performance, demonstrate to them that you will act upon their evaluations and take them seriously.
- Be prepared to modify teaching practice in order to take account of pupil evaluations of learning and teaching.
- Revisit pupil evaluations regularly with the pupil and discuss whether they can recognize any changes you may have made as a result of these.
- Involve pupils in planning the implementation of change following evaluations.
- Encourage pupils to discuss their evaluations with their peers and to identify how they may work together to improve their own and each others' performance.

Each of these principles requires regular review and reflection on the part of the teacher who is fully committed to pupil involvement, and each may be turned into a question upon which inquiry and reflection can be based. Case study 8.2 from a secondary school demonstrates how teachers in an English department supported each other in researching the impact of involving pupils in the planning of their own learning targets.

Case study 8.2 Barbara: researching classroom practice

Barbara is Head of English in a large inner-city comprehensive school. The school serves a catchment area, which includes a housing estate that has recently become home to a large number of families who have moved into the country from Eastern Europe. Within her department Barbara is responsible for the management of six teachers of varying experience and four teaching assistants, whose work is wholly within the department. For the past five terms the English department has been implementing a programme focusing on enabling pupils for whom English is an additional language to assess their own learning needs, to set targets for language-skills development and to evaluate the effectiveness of the teaching they receive in English lessons. At a recent departmental meeting it was suggested that it might be appropriate to conduct a small-scale inquiry to assess how well these pupil-involvement procedures were working. In order to do this Barbara, with the collaboration of her team, implemented a series of observations of lessons looking at the pupil involvement procedures being used.

The lesson observations developed for this purpose follow a set procedure. Prior to the lesson Barbara reads through the teacher's lesson plans and takes particular note of the targets set by individual pupils to support their own learning. Before the lesson begins, with the support of the class teacher, Barbara selects a pupil to help her with conducting the observation. With the agreement of all the pupils in the class Barbara discusses with this pupil the targets towards which pupils are working and the plans the teacher has made to address these targets. Both Barbara and the pupil observe the lesson, making particular note of whenever a pupil is working on a personal target. At the end of the lesson Barbara and the pupil who has been helping with the observation discuss with the whole class and the teacher what they have seen. They pay particular attention to examples where they have seen pupils working towards their individual targets. They spend time asking the pupils about how helpful they find it to have individual targets and to provide examples of when the teacher has taken actions which they find particularly helpful, and also to highlight anything which is not so helpful.

Barbara repeats this exercise with five different teachers. At the end of this process, during a department meeting the teachers discuss what has been learned. They evaluate this small-scale inquiry by using specific questions.

- What have we learned about the target setting system which involves pupils?
- What is the evidence for what we have learned?
- What does this mean to us as a department?
- What actions might we take in order to develop our practice?

Discussions have revealed several examples of good practice in encouraging pupils to focus upon their own learning needs in lessons. This is reassuring to staff and encourages them to consider how they might further develop the procedures. Following the department meeting the teachers discuss with the pupils in their classes what they have found out. They talk about how they wish to continue to build on the system and ask the pupils for any further suggestions they may have. These are noted and over the next few weeks the pupils are encouraged to see how their opinions and the observations made by their peers and by Barbara are being implemented.

In Case study 8.2 the teachers recognized the importance of evaluating the procedures they had adopted. Having given a commitment to pupil involvement they continued this through their own researching into the effectiveness of the pupil target-setting system. Furthermore, they embarked upon this activity with a commitment to implement change based upon their findings and to share their findings with the pupils. This procedure has been based upon both a commitment to professional development and a principle of respect for the pupils at the heart of the learning process. The time invested in setting up a relatively straightforward inquiry into classroom practice produced a number of positive outcomes. First, it reassured staff that their approach has been beneficial and is having a positive impact on the learning of pupils for whom English is an additional language. Second, it enabled teachers to reflect upon their practices and to consider how they may move forward in building upon these for the benefits of pupils. Third, it gave a positive message to pupils about the commitment of teachers to continue to address their needs and to assist them in overcoming difficulties with learning.

AVOIDING TOKENISM AND LEARNING MORE

Throughout this book we have endeavoured to give a positive message about the greater involvement of pupils in all aspects of their own learning. It would, however, be disingenuous to suggest that moves in this direction come without challenge. Our commitment to continue along a path to greater understanding of how pupils can take more responsibility for their own learning is well established, but we acknowledge that for many teachers and their pupils there are considerable difficulties to be overcome. It is these obstacles that we would suggest are most important in respect of setting a further research agenda.

For some pupils, and particularly those with special educational needs, difficulties with communication may prove problematic for their involvement in target setting. Similarly, the suggestible nature of some pupils who are keen to please their teachers, and who will therefore be easily led rather than making their own decisions, can create challenges. Both of these issues have already begun to attract the attention of teachers and researchers committed to understanding how greater pupil independence may be achieved. However, it is important to recognize the need to avoid tokenistic practices whereby pupil consultation becomes a blasé procedure undertaken in a superficial manner in order to satisfy school requirements or to falsely indicate a commitment to pupil involvement.

Much is to be learned from those teachers who, through their work with pupils with the most complex learning needs, have experimented with the use of augmentative forms of communication, such as symbol systems, in order to provide greater access to decision making (Hayes 2004). Similarly, teachers of children in the early years and especially those working in nursery settings have often made a commitment to developing environments and an ethos that encourages children to make decisions and choices from a very early age. Seemingly simple practices, such as offering choices about their play activities or developing circle activities with opportunities to listen to pupils talking about their ideas and experiences, may be critical in developing pupil confidence and self-esteem (Mortimer 2004). This kind of approach has often led to the implementation of procedures which, whilst being informal, are invaluable in ensuring that children gain confidence and encouragement as learners. As we have stated in this chapter, simply implementing procedures is not sufficient in terms of promoting greater understanding of what works in pupil involvement. This must be accompanied by a commitment to questioning and investigating the efficacy and practicability of systems.

Teachers are already raising questions and searching for solutions, which we should take as leading the way for future research agendas. Systematic inquiry into those approaches that enable pupils to feel good about learning and valued as individuals should be seen as a vital part of the education agenda in the immediate future.

SUMMARY

In this chapter we have:

- defined research and its value to classroom teachers
- considered how we might further investigate the efficacy of pupil involvement
- identified an agenda for practitioner research.

REFERENCES

Cordingley, P. (2004) 'Teachers Using Evidence: Using What We Know about Teaching and Learning to Reconceptualize Evidence-based Practice.' In G. Thomas and R. Pring (eds) *Evidence-Based Practice in Education*. Buckingham: Open University.

Hayes, J. (2004) 'Visual annual reviews: how to include pupils with learning difficulties in their educational reviews.' *Support for Learning 19*, 4, 175–180.

Lord Laming, (2009) *The Protection of Children in England: A Progress Report*. London: The Stationery Office.

Loughran, J. (1999) 'Researching Teaching for Understanding.' In J. Loughran (ed.) *Researching Teaching: Methodologies and Practices for Understanding Pedagogy*. London: Falmer Press.

Mortimer, H. (2004) 'Hearing children's voices in the early years.' *Support for Learning 19*, 4, 169–174.

Reitemeier, B. (2008) Letter written on behalf of the Children's Society to Lord Laming, 5th December. Available at www.childrenssociety.org.uk/resources/documents/Policy/12504_full.pdf, accessed on 8 September 2009.

Subject Index

Author Index